Read Alouds and Primary Sources

Editorial Offices: Glenview, Illinois • Parsippany, New Jersey • New York, New York
Sales Offices: Parsippany, New Jersey • Duluth, Georgia • Glenview, Illinois • Coppell, Texas • Ontario, California

www.sfsocialstudies.com

Program Authors

Dr. Candy Dawson Boyd
Professor, School of Education
Director of Reading Programs
St. Mary's College
Moraga, California

Dr. Geneva Gay
Professor of Education
University of Washington
Seattle, Washington

Rita Geiger
Director of Social Studies and Foreign Languages
Norman Public Schools
Norman, Oklahoma

Dr. James B. Kracht
Associate Dean for Undergraduate Programs and Teacher Education
College of Education
Texas A&M University
College Station, Texas

Dr. Valerie Ooka Pang
Professor of Teacher Education
San Diego State University
San Diego, California

Dr. C. Frederick Risinger
Director, Professional Development and Social Studies Education
Indiana University
Bloomington, Indiana

Sara Miranda Sanchez
Elementary and Early Childhood Curriculum Coordinator
Albuquerque Public Schools
Albuquerque, New Mexico

Contributing Authors

Dr. Carol Berkin
Professor of History
Baruch College and the Graduate Center
The City University of New York
New York, New York

Lee A. Chase
Staff Development Specialist
Chesterfield County Public Schools
Chesterfield County, Virginia

Dr. Jim Cummins
Professor of Curriculum
Ontario Institute for Studies in Education
University of Toronto
Toronto, Canada

Dr. Allen D. Glenn
Professor and Dean Emeritus
Curriculum and Instruction
College of Education
University of Washington
Seattle, Washington

Dr. Carole L. Hahn
Professor, Educational Studies
Emory University
Atlanta, Georgia

Dr. M. Gail Hickey
Professor of Education
Indiana University-Purdue University
Fort Wayne, Indiana

Dr. Bonnie Meszaros
Associate Director
Center for Economic Education and Entrepreneurship
University of Delaware
Newark, Delaware

ISBN 0-328-03780-X

1 2 3 4 5 6 7 8 9 10-V016-11 10 09 08 07 06 05 04 03 02

Contents

Unit 3

Unit 4

Unit 5

Unit 6

Unit 7

Unit 8

Unit 9

INTRODUCTION

The *Read Aloud and Primary Sources* anthology contains selections to accompany each unit of the pupil edition. These selections are to be read aloud to students to give them access to materials they might not be able to read independently. Hearing these selections read aloud will enrich the students' understanding of the unit topics.

What You'll Find Inside

One type of selection in this anthology is called a **Read Aloud**. The Read Aloud selections include a variety of genre:

- poems
- songs
- folk tales and myths
- novel excerpts
- short stories
- nonfiction articles

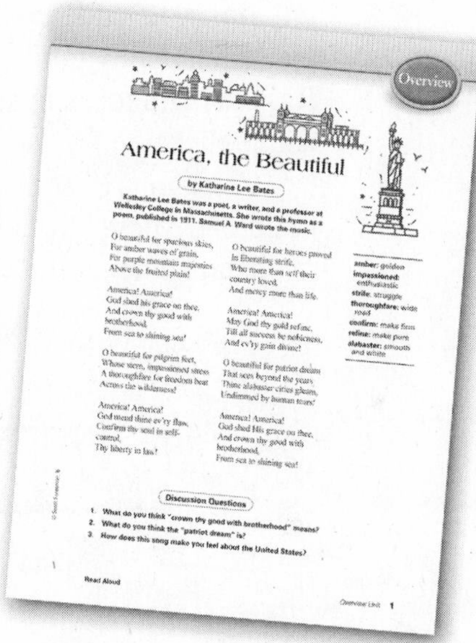

Overview

America, the Beautiful

by Katharine Lee Bates

Katharine Lee Bates was a poet, a writer, and a professor at Wellesley College in Massachusetts. She wrote this hymn as a poem, published in 1911. Samuel A. Ward wrote the music.

O beautiful for spacious skies,
For amber waves of grain,
For purple mountain majesties
Above the fruited plain!

America! America!
God shed his grace on thee,
And crown thy good with brotherhood,
From sea to shining sea!

O beautiful for pilgrim feet,
Whose stern, impassioned stress
A thoroughfare for freedom beat
Across the wilderness!

America! America!
God mend thine ev'ry flaw,
Confirm thy soul in self-control,
Thy liberty in law!

O beautiful for heroes proved
In liberating strife,
Who more than self their country loved,
And mercy more than life.

America! America!
May God thy gold refine,
Till all success be nobleness,
And ev'ry gain divine!

O beautiful for patriot dream
That sees beyond the years
Thine alabaster cities gleam,
Undimmed by human tears!

America! America!
God shed His grace on thee,
And crown thy good with brotherhood,
From sea to shining sea!

amber: golden
impassioned: enthusiastic
strife: struggle
thoroughfare: wide road
confirm: make firm
refine: make pure
alabaster: smooth and white

Discussion Questions

1. What do you think "crown thy good with brotherhood" means?
2. What do you think the "patriot dream" is?
3. How does this song make you feel about the United States?

Read Aloud

Overview Unit 1

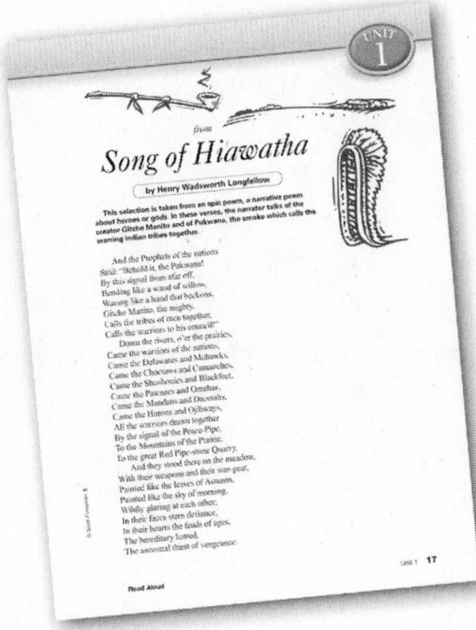

Unit 1

from

Song of Hiawatha

by Henry Wadsworth Longfellow

This selection is taken from an epic poem, a narrative poem about heroes or gods. In these verses, the narrator talks of the creator Gitche Manito and of Pukwana, the smoke which calls the warring Indian tribes together.

And the Prophets of the nations
Said: "Behold it, the Pukwana!
By this signal from afar off,
Bending like a wand of willow,
Waving like a hand that beckons,
Gitche Manito, the mighty,
Calls the tribes of men together,
Calls the warriors to his council!"
Down the rivers, o'er the prairies,
Came the warriors of the nations,
Came the Delawares and Mohawks,
Came the Choctaws and Camanches,
Came the Shoshonies and Blackfeet,
Came the Pawnees and Omahas,
Came the Mandans and Dacotahs,
Came the Hurons and Ojibways,
All the warriors drawn together
By the signal of the Peace-Pipe,
To the Mountains of the Prairie,
To the great Red Pipe-stone Quarry.
And they stood there on the meadow,
With their weapons and their war-gear,
Painted like the leaves of Autumn,
Painted like the sky of morning,
Wildly glaring at each other;
In their faces stern defiance,
In their hearts the feuds of ages,
The hereditary hatred,
The ancestral thirst of vengeance.

Unit 1 17

Read Aloud

The second type of selection in this anthology is called a **Primary Source**. Primary sources are materials that were written or created during the time period that is being studied. The Primary Source selections include materials such as these:

- historical documents
- newspaper articles
- diary or journal entries
- speeches
- letters
- first-person accounts
- interviews
- oral histories
- political cartoons
- photographs

The language used in some of the primary sources may be unfamiliar to students. To help them understand these selections, pause frequently during your oral reading to explain vocabulary. Restate main ideas in simpler language to help students' comprehension.

Certain primary sources use nonstandard spelling and grammar. These have been reproduced here without corrections to maintain authenticity.

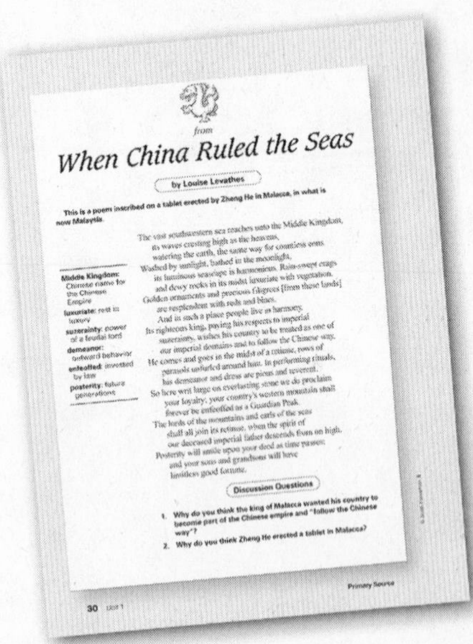

from

When China Ruled the Seas

by Louise Levathes

This is a poem inscribed on a tablet erected by Zheng He in Malacca, in what is now Malaysia.

The vast southwestern sea reaches unto the Middle Kingdom,
its waves cresting high as the heavens,
watering the earth, the same way for countless eons.
Washed by sunlight, bathed in the moonlight,
its luminous seascape is harmonious. Rain-swept crags
and dewy rocks in its midst luxuriate with vegetation.
Golden ornaments and precious filigrees [from these lands]
are resplendent with reds and blues.
And in such a place people live in harmony.
Its righteous king, paying his respects to imperial
suzerainty, wishes his country to be treated as one of
our imperial domains and to follow the Chinese way.
He comes and goes in the midst of a retinue, rows of
parasols unfurled around him. In performing rituals,
his demeanor and dress are pious and reverent.
So here writ large on everlasting stone we do proclaim
your loyalty; your country's western mountain shall
forever be enfeoffed as a Guardian Peak.
The lords of the mountains and earls of the seas
shall all join its retinue, when the spirit of
our deceased imperial father descends from on high.
Posterity will smile upon your deed as time passes;
and your sons and grandsons will have
limitless good fortune.

Middle Kingdom: Chinese name for the Chinese Empire
luxuriate: rest in luxury
suzerainty: power of a feudal lord
demeanor: outward behavior
enfeoffed: invested by law
posterity: future generations

Discussion Questions

1. **Why do you think the king of Malacca wanted his country to become part of the Chinese empire and "follow the Chinese way"?**
2. **Why do you think Zheng He erected a tablet in Malacca?**

30 Unit 1 Primary Source

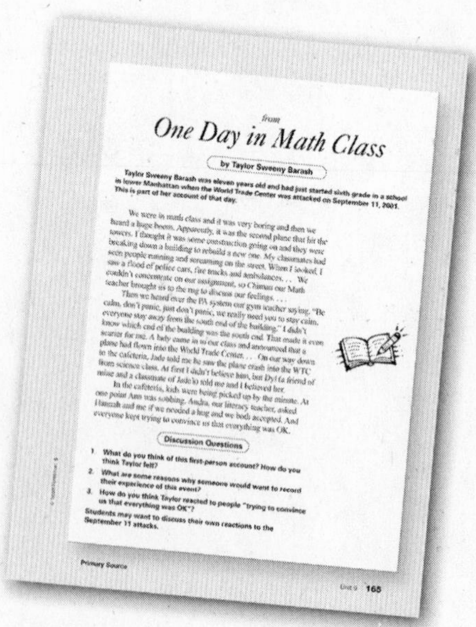

from

One Day in Math Class

by Taylor Sweeny Barash

Taylor Sweeny Barash was eleven years old and had just started sixth grade in a school in lower Manhattan when the World Trade Center was attacked on September 11, 2001. This is part of her account of that day.

We were in math class and it was very boring and then we heard a huge boom. Apparently, it was the second plane that hit the towers. I thought it was some construction going on and they were breaking down a building to rebuild a new one. My classmates had seen people running and screaming on the street. When I looked, I saw a flood of police cars, fire trucks and ambulances. . . We couldn't concentrate on our assignment, so Chiman our Math teacher brought us to the rug to discuss our feelings. . . .

Then we heard over the PA system our gym teacher saying, "Be calm, don't panic, just don't panic, we really need you to stay calm, everyone stay away from the south end of the building." I didn't know which end of the building was the south end. That made it even scarier for me. A lady came in to our class and announced that a plane had flown into the World Trade Center. . . . On our way down to the cafeteria, Jade told me he saw the plane crash into the WTC from science class. At first I didn't believe him, but Dyl (a friend of mine and a classmate of Jade's) told me and I believed her.

In the cafeteria, kids were being picked up by the minute. At one point Ann was sobbing. Andra, our literacy teacher, asked Hannah and me if we needed a hug and we both accepted. And everyone kept trying to convince us that everything was OK.

Discussion Questions

1. **What do you think of this first-person account? How do you think Taylor felt?**
2. **What are some reasons why someone would want to record their experience of this event?**
3. **How do you think Taylor reacted to people "trying to convince us that everything was OK"?**

Students may want to discuss their own reactions to the September 11 attacks.

Primary Source Unit 9 165

How to Use the Selections

Each anthology selection relates to a specific textbook topic. Corresponding pupil edition chapter and lesson references are provided in the Table of Contents. We recommend that each selection be read to students soon after they have read the related topic in the textbook. These features will help you present each selection:

- The introductory note for each selection provides background information to share with students about the piece.
- Vocabulary, located in the margin of the page on which each word appears, may be reviewed either before or during reading.
- Discussion questions following the selection provide a springboard for class discussion; further talk about the selection and its relationship to the textbook content is encouraged.
- Ideas for further investigation of a topic are sometimes suggested. When the reading level is appropriate, we recommend that students read the entire book from which the selection is taken on their own or that you read more of it aloud in class.

How to Connect School and Home

The anthology selections may also be used to involve parents or guardians in the learning process. Selections may be photocopied and sent home with students as a homework assignment. The student can briefly explain the related topic studied in class, the adult can read the introduction and selection aloud, and the adult and student can discuss the questions together.

from

Liliuokalani: Queen of Hawaii

by Mary Malone

In this excerpt, Liliuokalani, Hawaii's last queen, gives in to the American businessmen who want her to resign.

Most of Liliuokalani's own people did support her. They were even ready to fight for her. But the queen did not want anyone to fight. She spoke to her people from the palace balcony.

"Be patient," she said. "There must be no bloodshed. For my sake, go back to your homes."

Most of them did. But some were angry about the way the queen was being treated. This gave Liliuokalani's enemies an excuse to form the Committee of Public Safety. The committee members said they feared "rioting" by the native Hawaiians. They asked the American minister in Hawaii to land troops from an American ship in Honolulu harbor. He did so.

The next day the queen looked out and saw American marines outside her palace.

"What is the meaning of this?" she asked the leader of the committee, who had come to see her.

"We are asking you to resign," he replied. "We want a businessman like Sanford Dole to head the government."

"I will not resign," Liliuokalani said. The man pointed to the guards outside. Then the queen knew that if her own people tried to help her, some might be shot. She must give in to these men. Sadly, she sat down at her desk and wrote a short note to Mr. Dole. "I am resigning," Liliuokalani said, "because I am forced to do it. To avoid the loss of life . . . I yield."

Discussion Questions

1. **What did Liliuokalani care about at this critical time?**
2. **What do you think of Liliuokalani's actions?**

146 Unit 8

Read Aloud

ACKNOWLEDGMENTS

2 From "The Immigrant Experience," www.ellisisland.com.

4 From "A National Historic Landmark Also Known as the 'North Garrison,'" www.angelisland.org. Reprinted by permission.

7 From *Madam C.J. Walker* by A'Lelia Perry Bundles, pp. 63, 70, 71, 13, 14. Copyright © 1991 by Chelsea House Publishers. Reprinted by permission.

13 From "Mission: Recycle," www.kidsface.org. Reprinted by permission of Kids for a Clean Environment.

14 From *The Everglades: River of Grass* by Marjory Stoneman Douglas, pp. 5-6; 9-10.

21 From *Inca Town* by Fiona Macdonald, 1998.

23 From "Folio 2r: The Founding of the Tenochtitlan" from *The Essential Codex Mendoza* by Frances F. Berdan and Patricia Rieff Anawalt.

26 From *My Indian Boyhood* by Chief Luther Standing Bear, 1959, pp. 1-2; 5; 67.

28 From *The Travels of Marco Polo,* translated and edited by William Marsden; reedited by Thomas Wright, 1948, pp. 121-122, 96-97.

30 From *When China Ruled the Seas* translated by Chu HungLam and James Geiss, pp. 209-210.

32 From "To the Edge of the World!" from *The Viking News* by Rachel Wright.

34 From *Where do you think you're going Christopher Columbus?* by Jean Fritz, G.P.Putnam's Sons, 1980, pp. 70-71; 73.

36 From *Castaways: The Narrative of Alvar N'Òez Cabeza De Vaca* edited by Enrique PupoWalker, translated by Frances M. LÛpezMorillas, pp. 103-104, 106-107.

40 From *A Journey to the New World: The Diary of Remember Patience Whipple,* by Kathryn Lasky, 1996, pp. 3-7; 9-12.

47 From *Letters from New England* edited by Everett Emerson, pp. 46-47.

52 From *The Captive,* by Joyce Hansen, 1994, pp. 91-94.

54 From *Calico Bush* by Rachel Field, 1931, pp. 8-11.

61 Paul Horgan, *The Great River.* New York: Rinehart & Company, Inc. 1954, p. 285-286.

67 From *Johnny Tremain* by Esther Forbes, pp. 124-127.

80 From *The Adams Family Correspondence,* Vol I, edited by L.H. Butterfield, pp. 369-370.

82 From *The Winter of Red Snow,* by Kristiana Gregory, p 12.

90 From *Daniel Boone* by John Mason Brown, pp. 79-85.

97 From *Streams to the River, River to the Sea* by Scott O'Dell, pp. 74-79.

102 From *The Cherokee Removal,* 1838 by Glen Fleischmann, 1971, pp. 3-4; 67-70.

112 From *Davy Crocket: Defender of the Alamo* by William R. Sanford & Carl R. Green, pp. 38-41.

114 From *Levi Strauss: Blue Jean Tycoon* by Meish Goldish, pp. 21-27.

119 From *Steal Away* by Jennifer M. Armstrong, 1992, pp.82-85.

127 From *Angel of the Battlefield* by Ishbel Ross, 1956, pp. 31-35.

129 From *Virginia's General: Robert E. Lee and the Civil War* by Albert Marrin, 1994, pp. 184-186.

136 From *The West* by Geoffrey C. Ward, pp. 241, 243.

138 From *Sitting Bull: Sioux Leader* by Elizabeth Schleichert; Enslow Publishers, Inc, pp. 59-62. All rights reserved. Reprinted by permission.

140 From *Thomas Alva Edison* by Carole Greene, 1985, pp. 108-111.

142 Samuel Gompers.

146 From *Liliuokalani: Queen of Hawaii* by Mary Malone, pp. 59-60.

152 From *Crusade for Justice: The Autobiography of Ida B. Wells* edited by Alfreda M. Duster.

153 From Charles A. Lindbergh article, *The New York Times,* May 22, 1927.

157 From *My Secret War* by Mary Pope Osborne, pp. 26-29.

161 Malcolm X, *The Autobiography of Malcolm X.* New York: Grove Press, 1965, p. 275, 375.

162 From *Cesar Chavez: Man of Courage* by Florence White, pp. 83-88.

164 From "The End of the War to End Wars" from *The New York Times,* November 11, 1989.

165 "One Day in Math Class" by Taylor Sweeny Barash.

America, the Beautiful

by Katharine Lee Bates

Katharine Lee Bates was a poet, a writer, and a professor at Wellesley College in Massachusetts. She wrote this hymn as a poem, published in 1911. Samuel A. Ward wrote the music.

O beautiful for spacious skies,
For amber waves of grain,
For purple mountain majesties
Above the fruited plain!

America! America!
God shed his grace on thee,
And crown thy good with brotherhood,
From sea to shining sea!

O beautiful for pilgrim feet,
Whose stern, impassioned stress
A thoroughfare for freedom beat
Across the wilderness!

America! America!
God mend thine ev'ry flaw,
Confirm thy soul in self-control,
Thy liberty in law!

O beautiful for heroes proved
In liberating strife,
Who more than self their country loved,
And mercy more than life.

America! America!
May God thy gold refine,
Till all success be nobleness,
And ev'ry gain divine!

O beautiful for patriot dream
That sees beyond the years
Thine alabaster cities gleam,
Undimmed by human tears!

America! America!
God shed His grace on thee,
And crown thy good with brotherhood,
From sea to shining sea!

amber: golden
impassioned: enthusiastic
strife: struggle
thoroughfare: wide road
confirm: make firm
refine: make pure
alabaster: smooth and white

Discussion Questions

1. **What do you think "crown thy good with brotherhood" means?**
2. **What do you think the "patriot dream" is?**
3. **How does this song make you feel about the United States?**

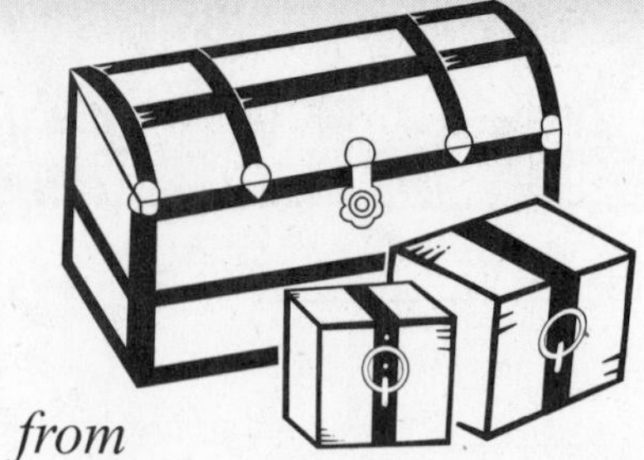

from

Ellis Island History

During the early part of the twentieth century, millions of people left their homes in Europe and the Middle East to sail for the United States in hopes of finding a better life. Many of them came into the United States through Ellis Island in New York Harbor. This article comes from the Ellis Island Immigration Museum's web site.

Cossacks: Russian soldiers

caste: social levels that cannot be changed

steerage: the lower, least expensive decks of ships

When the great steamships of the early 20th century sailed into New York Harbor, the faces of a thousand nations were on board. A broad, beaming, multicolored parade, these were the immigrants of the world: there were Russian Jews with fashioned beards, Irish farmers whose hands were weathered like the land they had left, Greeks in kilts and slippers, Italians with sharp moustaches, Cossacks with fierce swords, English in short knickers, and Arabs in long robes. The old world lay behind them. Ahead was a new life, huge and promising. Gone were the monarchies and kings, the systems of caste and peasantry, of famine and numbing poverty. But also left behind were friends and family, as well as tradition and customs generations old. As anchors slid into harbor silt, and whistles blew in rival chorus, this multitude clambered up from the steerage decks to fashion in their minds forever their first glimpse of America. The city skyline loomed over them like a great, blocky mountain range. Poet Walt Whitman described New York as the "City of the World (for all of races are here, all the lands of the earth make contributions here:) City of the sea! City of hurried and glittering tides! City whose gleeful tides continually rush and recede, whirling in and out with eddies and foam! City of wharves and stores—city of tall facades of marble and iron! Proud and passionate city—mettlesome, mad, extravagant, city!" Below, the harbor teemed with activity as tugboats churned river water and dockhands wrestled cargo at America's most populous port. Across the Hudson stood the mythic vision of America: salt-green and copper-clad, the Statue of Liberty offered a mute but powerful welcome. In the shadow of all the activity, on the New Jersey side of the river, were the red brick buildings of Ellis Island. The four towers of its largest building rose over 140 feet into the air, punctuating its already intimidating facade with ramrod sternness.

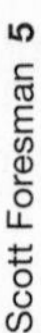

This was an official building, a place of rules and questions, of government and bureaucracy, where five thousand people a day were processed.

Men usually emigrated first, to find jobs and housing. Later they would send for their wives, children, and parents as part of the largest mass movement of people in world history. In all, close to 60 million people sought to find new opportunities during the 19th and early 20th centuries. Some merely crossed borders in Europe but many headed for countries such as Australia, New Zealand, Brazil, Argentina, and Canada. The majority, however, headed to the United States where they heard promise of jobs, freedom, and a fortune to be made. . . .

Today's visitors to Ellis Island, although unencumbered by bundled possessions and the harrowing memory of a transatlantic journey, retrace the steps of twelve million immigrants who approached America's "front doors to freedom" in the early twentieth century. Ellis Island receives today's arriving ferry passengers as it did hundreds of thousands of new arrivals between 1897 and 1938. In place of the business-like machinery of immigration inspection, the restored Main Hall now houses the Ellis Island Immigration Museum, dedicated to commemorating the immigrants' stories of trepidation and triumph, courage and rejection, and the lasting image of the American dream.

During its peak years—1892 to 1924—Ellis Island received thousands of immigrants a day. Each was scrutinized for disease or disability as the long line of hopeful new arrivals made their way up the steep stairs to the great, echoing Registry Room. Over 100 million Americans can trace their ancestry in the United States to a man, woman, or child whose name passed from a steamship manifest sheet to an inspector's record book in the great Registry Room at Ellis Island.

With restrictions on immigration in the 1920s Ellis Island's population dwindled, and the station finally closed its doors in 1954. Its grand brick and limestone buildings gradually deteriorated in the fierce weather of New York Harbor. Concern about this vital part of America's immigrant history led to the inclusion of Ellis Island as part of Statue of Liberty National Monument in 1965. Private citizens mounted a campaign to preserve the Island, and one of the most ambitious restoration projects in American history returned Ellis Island's Main Building to its former grandeur in September, 1990.

Discussion Question

What do you think Ellis Island was like, with so many people from so many different countries going through every day?

from

Angel Island Immigration Station

Angel Island Immigration Station, in San Francisco Bay, usually detained Asian immigrants rather than process their entry quickly as at Ellis Island. This piece comes from the Angel Island Web site.

The Purpose of the Station

In 1905, construction of an Immigration Station began in the area known as China Cove. Surrounded by public controversy from its inception, the station was finally put into operation in 1910. Anticipated as the "Ellis Island of the West," it was designed to handle a flood of European immigrants who were expected to begin arriving in California once the Panama Canal was opened. International events after 1914, including the outbreak of World War I, canceled the expected rush of Europeans.

Instead, the majority of immigrants to America via the West Coast were from Asia. Like their European counterparts entering at New York City, they hoped to escape the economic or political hardships of the homelands. On Ellis Island, immigrants were processed through within hours or days; on Angel Island, they spent weeks or months.

This facility was primarily a detention center. Beginning with the Chinese Exclusion Act of 1882, a series of restrictive laws had prohibited the immigration of certain nationalities and social classes of Asians. Although all Asians were affected, the greatest impact was on the Chinese. In fact, more than 70 percent of the immigrants detained on Angel Island were Chinese.

Immigration Background

The first Chinese entered California in 1848, and within a few years, thousands more came, lured by the promise of Gam Sann or "Gold Mountain." Soon, discriminatory legislation forced them out of the gold fields and into low-paying, menial jobs. They laid tracks for the Central Pacific Railroad, reclaimed swamp land in the Sacramento delta, developed shrimp and abalone fisheries, and provided cheap labor wherever there was work no other group wanted or needed. . . .

When it opened in 1910, the new detention facility on Angel Island was considered ideal because of its isolation. There were buildings to house and care for detainees, a pier, and regular boat service to the mainland. During the next 30 years, this was the point of entry for most Chinese immigrants and approximately 175,000 came to Angel Island. The average detention was two to three weeks, but many stayed for several months and a few were forced to remain on the island for nearly two years.

Some detainees expressed their feelings in poetry that they brushed or carved onto the wooden walls of the detention center. Others simply waited, hoping for a favorable response to their appeals, but fearing deportation. Many of the poems that were carved into the walls of the center are still legible today. Others were documented through the efforts of two detainees, Smiley Jann and Tet Yee in 1931–32, who copied down the poetry while they awaited disposition of their cases.

In 1940, the government decided to abandon the Immigration Station on Angel Island. . . .

Creation of the Immigration Museum

After the war, the Immigration Station was abandoned and fell into disrepair. Like many other unused buildings on Angel Island, the detention barracks was scheduled for destruction in 1970. Prior to demolition, Park Ranger Alexander Weiss toured the building with flashlight in hand and noted the calligraphy carved in the walls. Through his efforts and those of Paul Chow and the Angel Island Immigration Station Historical Advisory Committee (AIISHAC), the dilapidated barracks was saved from demolition and special legislation was passed granting $250,000 to preserve and restore the barracks.

A museum has been established in the old barracks building. It includes a re-creation of one of the dormitories, and features some of the poems that were carved into the station's walls.

Discussion Questions

1. **Do you think it was a good idea to have immigrants stay at Angel Island for weeks or months? Why or why not?**
2. **What do you think the detainees' poems would be like?**

from

John F. Kennedy's Inaugural Address

In January of 1961, the U.S. felt threatened by communism in the Soviet Union and was in a "Cold War" with that country. This is part of the speech John Kennedy gave on the day he became president.

In your hands, my fellow citizens, more than mine, will rest the final success or failure of our course. Since this country was founded, each generation of Americans has been summoned to give testimony to its national loyalty. The graves of young Americans who answered the call to service surround the globe.

Now the trumpet summons us again—not as a call to bear arms, though arms we need—not as a call to battle, though embattled we are—but a call to bear the burden of a long twilight struggle, year in and year out, "rejoicing in hope, patient in tribulation"—a struggle against the common enemies of man: tyranny, poverty, disease and war itself.

Can we forge against these enemies a grand and global alliance, North and South, East and West, that can assure a more fruitful life for all mankind? Will you join in that historic effort?

In the long history of the world, only a few generations have been granted the role of defending freedom in its hour of maximum danger. I do not shrink from this responsibility—I welcome it. I do not believe that any of us would exchange places with any other people or any other generation. The energy, the faith, the devotion which we bring to this endeavor will light our country and all who serve it—and the glow from that fire can truly light the world.

And so, my fellow Americans: ask not what your country can do for you—ask what you can do for your country.

My fellow citizens of the world: ask not what America will do for you, but what together we can do for the freedom of man.

Finally, whether you are citizens of America or citizens of the world, ask of us here the same high standards of strength and sacrifice which we ask of you. With a good conscience our only sure reward, with history the final judge of our deeds, let us go forth to lead the land we love, asking His blessing and His help, but knowing that here on earth God's work must truly be our own.

Discussion Question

What does Kennedy mean by "ask of us here the same high standards of strength and sacrifice which we ask of you"?

from

speeches by Madam C. J. Walker

Madam Walker encouraged African American women to start their own businesses. These excerpts are from speeches to several different groups, including the National Negro Business League.

"I am not merely satisfied in making money for myself, for I am endeavoring to provide employment for hundreds of the women of my race. I had little or no opportunity when I started out in life, having been left an orphan. . . . I had to make my own living and my own opportunity! But I made it! That is why I want to say to every Negro woman present, don't sit down and wait for the opportunities to come. . . . Get up and make them!"

"Perseverance is my motto. It laid the Atlantic cable. It gave us the telegraph, telephone, and wireless. It gave to the world an Abraham Lincoln, and to a race freedom. It gave to the Negro Booker T. Washington and Tuskegee Institute. It made Frederick Douglass the great orator that he was, and it gave to the race Paul Laurence Dunbar and to poetry a new song."

"If I have accomplished anything in life it is because I have been willing to work hard. I never yet started anything doubtingly, and I have always believed in keeping at things with a vim. There is no royal flower-strewn road to success, and if there is I have not found it, for what success I have obtained is the result of many sleepless nights and real hard work."

"I am a woman who came from the cotton fields of the South. I was promoted from there to the washtub. Then I was promoted to the cook kitchen, and from there *I promoted myself* into the business of manufacturing hair goods and preparations. I have built my own factory on my own ground."

"My object in life is not simply to make money for myself or to spend it on myself. I love to use a part of what I make in trying to help others."

Discussion Questions

1. **Did Madam Walker have reasons to be honest or dishonest?**
2. **How was Madam Walker like Thomas Edison in her philosophy or character?**

from

Carver's testimony about the peanut

George Washington Carver went to Congress in 1921 to tell the House Ways and Means Committee about the many uses of the peanut. He brought samples of the products to show the representatives and answered their questions.

Mr. Chairman, I have been asked by the United Peanut Growers' Association to tell you something about the possibility of the peanut and its possible extension. I come from Tuskegee, Ala. I am engaged in agricultural research work, and I have given some attention to the peanut, but not as much as I expect to give. I have given a great deal of time to the sweet potato and allied southern crops. I am especially interested in southern crops and their possibilities, and the peanut comes in, I think, for one of the most remarkable crops that we are all acquainted with. It will tell us a number of things that we do not already know, and you will also observe that it has possibilities that we are just beginning to find out. . . .

This is the crushed cake, which has a great many possibilities. I simply call attention to that. The crushed cake may be used in all sorts of combinations—for flours and meals and breakfast foods and a great many things that I have not time to touch upon just now.

Then we have the hulls, which are ground and made into a meal for burnishing tin plate. It has a very important value in that direction, and more of it is going to be used as the tin-plate manufacturers understand its value. . . .

This is another confection. It is peanuts covered with chocolate. As I passed through Greensboro, S.C., I noticed in one of the stores that this was displayed on the market, and, as it is understood better, more of it is going to be made up into this form.

Here is a breakfast food. I am very sorry that you can not taste this, so I will taste it for you.

Now this is a combination and, by the way, one of the finest breakfast foods that you or anyone else has ever seen. It is a combination of the sweet potato and the peanut. . . .

Here is the original salted peanut, for which there is an increasing demand, and here is a very fine peanut bar. The peanut bar is coming into prominence in a way that very few of us recognize, and the manufacturers of this peanut bar have learned that it is a very difficult matter to get a binder for it, something to stick it together. That is found in the sweet potato sirup. The sweet potato sirup makes one of the best binders of anything yet found. So in comes the sweet potato again.

Then we have the peanut stock food. This is No. 1, which consists of the ground hay, ground into meal, much the same as our alfalfa hay, which has much of the same composition as our alfalfa hay, and we are going to use more of it just as soon as we find out its value. So that nothing about the peanut need to be thrown away.

Here is peanut meal No. 2. That can be used for making flours and confections and candies, and doughnuts, and Zu-Zus and ginger bread and all sorts of things of that kind. . . .

Now there is an entirely new thing in the way of combinations. It is a new thing for making ice cream. It is a powder made largely from peanuts, with a little sweet potato injected into it to give it the necessary consistency. But it is far ahead of any flavoring yet found for ice cream. It is a very new product that is going to have considerable value. . . .

Here is breakfast food No. 5. That contains more protein than any of the others. One of them is a diabetic food. If any of you are suffering from that disease, you will find one of these breakfast foods very valuable, because it contains such a small amount of starch and sugar. . . .

Now, I want very hastily to bring before you another phase of the peanut industry which I think is well worth considering. Here a short time ago, or some months ago, we found how to extract milk from peanuts. Here is a bottle of milk that is extracted from peanuts. Now, it is absolutely impossible to tell that milk from cow's milk in looks and general appearance. This is normal milk. The cream rises on it the same as on cow's milk, and in fact it has much of the same composition as cow's milk.

Here is a bottle of full cream. That cream is very rich in fats, and can be used the same as the cream from cow's milk.

Discussion Questions

1. **Which, if any, of these peanut products do you eat? Which are popular in the United States today?**
2. **What do you think about all these uses for peanuts?**

Act of Congress to set aside Yellowstone as a public park

This is the law passed by Congress in 1872 that established Yellowstone Park as the first national park in the United States.

spoliation: spoiling
retention: keeping
wanton: irresponsible
expended: spent

Be it enacted by the Senate and House of Representatives of the United States of America in Congress assembled, That the tract of land in the Territories of Montana and Wyoming, lying near the head-waters of the Yellowstone river, . . . is hereby reserved and withdrawn from settlement, occupancy, or sale under the laws of the United States, and dedicated and set apart as a public park or pleasuring-ground for the benefit and enjoyment of the people; and all persons who shall locate or settle upon or occupy the same, or any part thereof, except as hereinafter provided, shall be considered trespassers and removed therefrom.

Sec. 2. That said public park shall be under the exclusive control of the Secretary of the Interior, whose duty it shall be, as soon as practicable, to make and publish such rules and regulations as he may deem necessary or proper for the care and management of the same. Such regulations shall provide for the preservation, from injury or spoliation, of all timber, mineral deposits, natural curiosities, or wonders within said park, and their retention in their natural condition. . . . He shall provide against the wanton destruction of the fish and game found within said park, and against their capture or destruction for the purposes of merchandise or profit. He shall also cause all persons trespassing upon the same after the passage of this act to be removed therefrom, and generally shall be authorized to take all such measures as shall be necessary or proper to fully carry out the objects and purposes of this act.

Approved, March 1, 1872.

Discussion Questions

1. **Do you think that it is important to keep the park in its "natural condition"? Why or why not?**
2. **What is your opinion about setting aside certain areas as national parks?**

Encourage students to use the Internet to find out about Yellowstone and other national parks.

Speech by Theodore Roosevelt at Grand Canyon

Theodore Roosevelt was known for his adventurousness, love of the wilderness, and physical courage. He made this speech at the Grand Canyon in Arizona in 1903.

irrigation: transportation of water through arid land

sublimity: nobility

speculator: buyer/seller of property

Mr. Governor, and you, my fellow citizens:

I am glad to be in Arizona to-day. From Arizona many gallant men came into the regiment which I had the honor to command. Arizona sent men who won glory on fought fields, and men to whom came a glorious and an honorable death fighting for the flag of their country. . . .

I have never been in Arizona before. It is one of the regions from which I expect most development through the wise action of the National Congress in passing the irrigation act. The first and biggest experiment now in view under that act is the one that we are trying in Arizona. I look forward to the effects of irrigation partly as applied by and through the government, still more as applied by individuals, and especially by associations of individuals, profiting by the example of the government, and possibly by help from it—I look forward to the effects of irrigation as being of greater consequence to all this region of country in the next fifty years than any other material movement whatsoever.

In the Grand Canyon, Arizona has a natural wonder which, so far as I know, is, in kind, absolutely unparalleled throughout the rest of the world. I want to ask you to do one thing in connection with it, in your own interest and in the interest of the country—to keep this great wonder of nature as it now is. I was delighted to learn of the wisdom of the Santa Fe railroad people in deciding not to build their hotel on the brink of the canyon. I hope you will not have a building of any kind, not a summer cottage, a hotel, or anything else, to mar the wonderful grandeur, the sublimity, the great loneliness and beauty of the canyon. Leave it as it is. You cannot improve on it. The ages have been at work on it, and man can only mar it. What you can do is to keep it for your children, your children's children and for all who come after you, as one of the great sights which every American, if he can travel at all, should see. . . .

If you deal with irrigation, apply it under circumstances that will make it of benefit, not to the speculator who hopes to get profit out of it for two or three years, but handle it so that it will be of use to the home-maker, to the man who comes to live here, and to have his children stay after him. Keep the forest in the same way. Preserve the forests by use; preserve them for the ranchman and the stockman, for the people of the Territory, for the people of the region round about. Preserve them for that use, but use them so that they will not be squandered, that they will not be wasted, so that they will be of benefit to the Arizona of 1953 as well as the Arizona of 1903. . . .

I believe in you. I am glad to see you. I wish you well with all my heart, and I know that your future will justify all the hopes we have.

Discussion Questions

1. **Why do you think Roosevelt wanted the Grand Canyon to be left as it was?**
2. **Do you think the Grand Canyon area should be kept "for your children, your children's children and for all who come after you"? Why or why not?**

Have students use the Internet or travel books to find out if over the years the people of Arizona have followed Roosevelt's advice about building near the Grand Canyon.

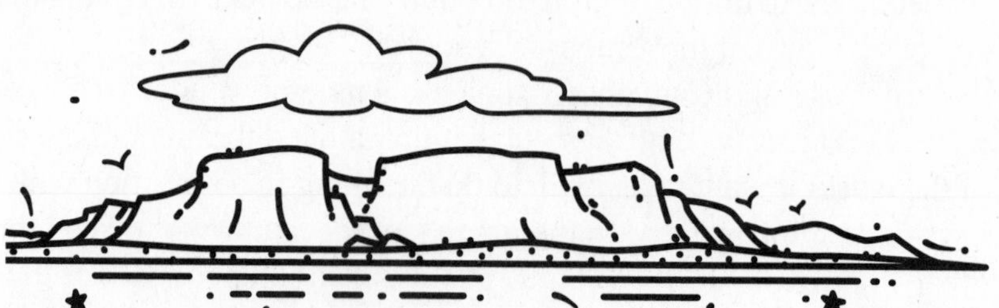

Mission: Recycle

This article comes from the online newsletter of Kids for a Clean Environment, an environmental group started by children.

Have you ever thought about where your homework paper goes when you are finished with the assignment? Do you simply throw that paper away? Or have you ever thought about what ever happens to the old toys when you outgrew them? Did you throw them away too when you cleaned out your room? What happens to the millions and millions of tons of waste thrown out by people every day? Well, all that trash is picked up from your house or school and taken to a landfill—a landfill that used to be part of nature's landscape. A landfill that sometimes, if old, seeps toxic waste into nearby water tables. A landfill that entombs a mountain of waste—unless, of course, if you recycle. . . .

According to Melissa Poe, the founder of Kids For A Clean Environment, ". . . it is so important to complete the recycling process—to not just recycle but to also reduce, reuse, and purchase recycled products as well as products packed in recycled materials!" This is the concept of the "little r & r" program which has an emphasis on closing the recycling loop by purchasing products made from recycled materials such as paper. "This is a very important step," explains Melissa, "because you can recycle all day long but unless someone is putting to use the material you recycled then it is just going to sit there until it is eventually thrown away."

Closing the recycling loop is very simple. First, you can recycle items from your home or school such as your school papers and your aluminum soda cans. You can also reuse items. . . . And when you are shopping or helping your parents shop, look for and show them the "chasing arrows" recycling symbol. . . .

Remember, just because you throw something away doesn't mean it has gone away. You have just moved it to a different location! So put it to good use, recycle it instead!

Discussion Questions

1. **Why do you think this article was written?**
2. **Do you recycle? Do you reuse items? How?**

from

The Everglades: River of Grass

by Marjorie Stoneman Douglas

Marjorie Stoneman Douglas went to college in the early 1900s, something few American women were able to do at that time. She lived to be 108 years old. This is an excerpt from her book about protecting the Everglades.

Note that when Douglas says *discovery,* she means "the European discovery of the Americas."

appendage: something attached to a main structure, as an arm or a leg is attached to the human body

I. The Name

There are no other Everglades in the world.

They are, they have always been, one of the unique regions of the earth, remote, never wholly known. Nothing anywhere else is like them: their vast glittering openness, wider than the enormous visible round of the horizon, the racing free saltness and sweetness of their massive winds, under the dazzling blue heights of space. They are unique also in the simplicity, the diversity, the related harmony of the forms of life they enclose. The miracle of the light pours over the green and brown expanse of saw grass and of water, shining and slow-moving below, the grass and water that is the meaning and the central fact of the Everglades of Florida. It is a river of grass.

The great pointed paw of the state of Florida, familiar as the map of North America itself, of which it is the most noticeable appendage, thrusts south, farther south than any other part of the mainland of the United States. Between the shining aquamarine waters of the Gulf of Mexico and the roaring deep-blue waters of the north-surging Gulf Stream, the shaped land points toward Cuba

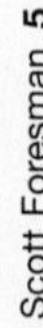

and the Caribbean. It points toward and touches within one degree of the tropics.

More than halfway down that thrusting sea-bound peninsula nearly everyone knows the lake that is like a great hole in that pawing shape, Lake Okeechobee, the second largest body of fresh water, it is always said, "within the confines of the United States." Below that lie the Everglades.

They have been called "the mysterious Everglades" so long that the phrase is a meaningless platitude. For four hundred years after the discovery they seemed more like a fantasy than a simple geographic and historic fact. Even the men who in the later years saw them more clearly could hardly make up their minds what the Everglades were or how they could be described, or what use could be made of them. They were mysterious then. They are mysterious still to everyone by whom their fundamental nature is not understood. . . .

platitude: dull expression
fundamental: basic

II. The Grass

The Everglades begin at Lake Okeechobee.

That is the name later Indians gave the lake, a name almost as recent as the word "Everglades." It means "Big Water." Everybody knows it.

Yet few have any idea of those pale, seemingly illimitable waters. Over the shallows, often less than a foot deep but seven hundred fifty or so square miles in actual area, the winds in one gray swift moment can shatter the reflections of sky and cloud whiteness standing still in that shining, polished, shimmering expanse. A boat can push for hours in a day of white sun through the short, crisp lake waves and there will be nothing to be seen anywhere but the brightness where the color of the water and the color of the sky become one. Men out of sight of land can stand in it up to their armpits and slowly "walk in" their long nets to the waiting boats. An everglade kite and his mate, questing in great solitary circles, rising and dipping and rising again on the wind currents, can look down all day long at the water faintly green with floating water lettuce or marked by thin standing lines of reeds, utter their sharp goat cries, and be seen and heard by no one at all.

There are great shallow islands, all brown reeds or shrubby trees thick in the water. There are masses of water weeds and hyacinths and flags rooted so long they seem solid earth, yet there is nothing but lake bottom to stand on. There the egret and the white ibis and the glossy ibis and the little blue herons in their thousands nested and circled and fed.

A long northeast wind, a "norther," can lash all that still surface to dirty vicious gray and white, over which the rain mists shut down like stained rolls of wool, so that from the eastern sand rim under dripping cypresses or the west ridge with its live oaks, no one would guess that all that waste of empty water stretched there but for the long monotonous wash of waves on unseen marshy shores.

Saw grass reaches up both sides of that lake in great enclosing arms, so that it is correct to say that the Everglades are there also. But south, southeast and southwest, where the lake water slopped and seeped and ran over and under the rock and soil, the greatest mass of the saw grass begins. It stretches as it always has stretched, in one thick enormous curving river of grass, to the very end. This is the Everglades.

It reaches one hundred miles from Lake Okeechobee to the Gulf of Mexico, fifty, sixty, even seventy miles wide. No one has ever fought his way along its full length. Few have ever crossed the northern wilderness of nothing but grass. Down that almost invisible slope the water moves. The grass stands. Where the grass and the water are there is the heart, the current, the meaning of the Everglades.

The grass and the water together make the river as simple as it is unique. There is no other river like it. Yet within that simplicity, enclosed within the river and bordering and intruding on it from each side, there is subtlety and diversity, a crowd of changing forms, of thrusting teeming life. And all that becomes the region of the Everglades.

Discussion Questions

1. **Did Douglas mean to inform or to persuade her readers?**
2. **How does this excerpt help you understand why Marjorie Stoneman Douglas fought to protect the Everglades?**

from

Song of Hiawatha

by Henry Wadsworth Longfellow

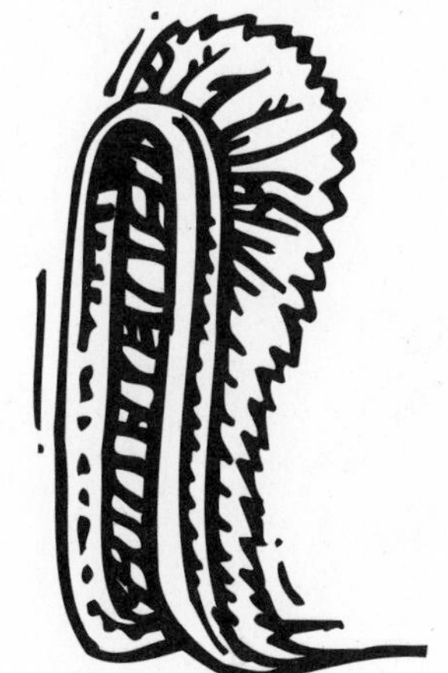

This selection is taken from an epic poem, a narrative poem about heroes or gods. In these verses, the narrator talks of the creator Gitche Manito and of Pukwana, the smoke which calls the warring Indian tribes together.

And the Prophets of the nations
Said: "Behold it, the Pukwana!
By this signal from afar off,
Bending like a wand of willow,
Waving like a hand that beckons,
Gitche Manito, the mighty,
Calls the tribes of men together,
Calls the warriors to his council!"
Down the rivers, o'er the prairies,
Came the warriors of the nations,
Came the Delawares and Mohawks,
Came the Choctaws and Camanches,
Came the Shoshonies and Blackfeet,
Came the Pawnees and Omahas,
Came the Mandans and Dacotahs,
Came the Hurons and Ojibways,
All the warriors drawn together
By the signal of the Peace-Pipe,
To the Mountains of the Prairie,
To the great Red Pipe-stone Quarry.
And they stood there on the meadow,
With their weapons and their war-gear,
Painted like the leaves of Autumn,
Painted like the sky of morning,
Wildly glaring at each other;
In their faces stern defiance,
In their hearts the feuds of ages,
The hereditary hatred,
The ancestral thirst of vengeance.

Gitche Manito, the mighty,
The creator of the nations,
Looked upon them with compassion,
With paternal love and pity;
Looked upon their wrath and wrangling
But as quarrels among children,
But as feuds and fights of children!
Over them he stretched his right hand,
To subdue their stubborn natures,
To allay their thirst and fever,
By the shadow of his right hand;
Spake to them with voice majestic
As the sound of far-off waters,
Falling into deep abysses,
Warning, chiding, spake in this wise:—
"O my children! My poor children!
Listen to the words of wisdom,
Listen to the words of warning,
From the lips of the Great Spirit,
From the Master of Life, who made you!
"I have given you lands to hunt in,
I have given you streams to fish in,
I have given you bear and bison,
I have given you roe and reindeer,
I have given you brant and beaver,
Filled the marshes full of wild-fowl,
Filled the rivers full of fishes;
Why then are you not contented?
Why then will you hunt each other?
"I am weary of your quarrels,
Weary of your wars and bloodshed,
Weary of your prayers for vengeance,
Of your wranglings and dissensions;
All your strength is in your union,
All your danger is in discord;
Therefore be at peace henceforward,
And as brothers live together.

Discussion Questions

1. **Does the writer of the poem have firsthand knowledge of the events or does he draw on other sources? Explain your answer.**
2. **Why do you think it was important for the different tribes to come together?**

Students may want to read the entire poem, "The Song of Hiawatha.

from

Cliff Palace

This description of the Cliff Palace at Mesa Verde National Park, from the National Park Service Web site, tells the story of the discovery of the site as well as giving information about its history. Tell students that because the Cliff Palace is 7,000 feet above sea level, only tourists who are physically fit can climb up to it. The Sun Temple, across the canyon from the palace, is a row of three stone-walled squares, the left of which contains a pattern like the sun. Its entry faces the southern cliff edge.

On December 18th, 1888, two cowboys, Richard Wetherill and his brother-in-law Charlie Mason, were riding across the mesa top looking for stray cattle. At the edge of the pinyon and juniper forest surrounding them lay a vast canyon near Sun Temple. Through the blowing snow they could distinguish something in the cliffs which looked like "a magnificent city." These ranchers from the Mancos Valley east of the park may have been the first white men to see what they called "Cliff Palace." After further exploration, they entered the dwelling and made a small collection of artifacts before leaving for the day. In the next 18 years these same men, as well as various exploring parties and tourist groups, made expeditions into Mesa Verde.

Many of the early visitors to the Mesa Verde area camped in the dwellings for days or weeks at a time while they were sightseeing or looking for cattle. Because there were no laws protecting such sites at the time, they often removed artifacts or defaced certain sections of the site. Protection for the dwellings came with the establishment of Mesa Verde in 1906, yet it was not until 1909 that Jesse Walter Fewkes of the Smithsonian Institution excavated and first stabilized Cliff Palace. . . . [The rock] is cliffhouse sandstone, geologically deposited during the Cretaceous Period some 78 million years ago. Since sandstone is very porous material, moisture seeps right down through it. Beneath the layer of sandstone, however, is a layer of shale through which the moisture cannot penetrate. In the winter months, when the moisture freezes and expands, chunks of sandstone are cracked and loosened. Later these pieces collapse, forming alcoves. . . .

The majority of alcoves are small crevices of ledges able to accommodate only a few small rooms. Very few are large enough to house a dwelling the size of Cliff Palace. Recent studies reveal that Cliff Palace contained 151 rooms and 23 kivas and had a population of 100–150 people. Out of the nearly 600 cliff dwellings concentrated within the boundaries of the park, 75% contain only 1–5 rooms each, and many are single room storage units. If you visit Cliff Palace you will be entering an exceptionally large dwelling which may have had special significance even for the original occupants.

The people who lived in Mesa Verde are sometimes referred to as the "Anasazi," a Navajo Indian word meaning "ancient ones" or "ancient foreigners." In recognition that the people who once lived here are not only the ancestors of some of the Navajo, but also ancestral to most tribes living in the southwest, we now refer to the ancient people of Mesa Verde as the Ancestral Puebloan people. There are 24 tribes that affirm an ancestral affiliation with Mesa Verde National Park. Tribes affiliated with the park include all of the pueblos of New Mexico, the Hopi tribe in Arizona, as well as the Ute and Navajo peoples.

The Ancestral Puebloan people moved up onto the mesa somewhere around AD 500. Although they used the cliff alcoves consistently throughout the time they were in the area, they did not build the cliff dwellings as such until around AD 1200. The dwellings represent a massive construction project, yet the people lived in them only about 75 to 100 years. By AD 1300 they had migrated on to other areas to the south. As you walk through Cliff Palace, keep in mind that this structure continues to hold many secrets which archeologists will never be able to unravel. For all of our advanced research and knowledge, we cannot answer certain basic questions about these ancient residents. Although we have many theories about why they left their homes, we really do not know the exact reason why they moved on.

Discussion Questions

1. **What advantages did the Cliff Palace offer the Anasazi?**
2. **What are some reasons why the Anasazi might have abandoned their homes and moved southward only about 75 to 100 years after their huge Mesa Verde construction project?**

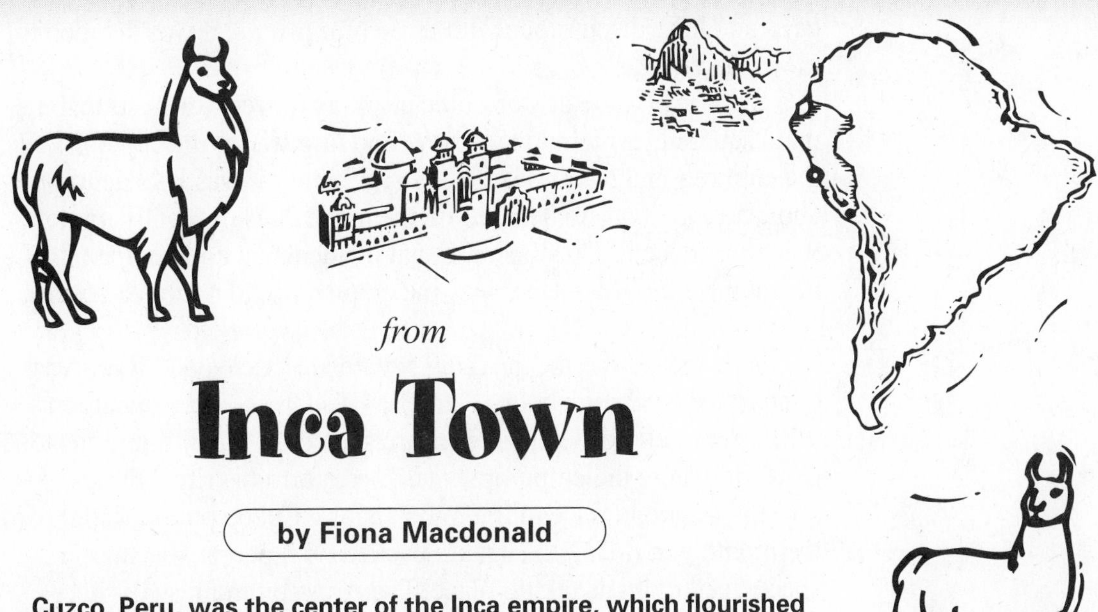

from

Inca Town

by Fiona Macdonald

Cuzco, Peru, was the center of the Inca empire, which flourished in South America from about 1200 until the Spanish conquest in 1533. Cuzco is far inland from Lima, Peru's modern-day capital; it is high in the Andes Mountains and difficult to reach. This "guided tour" explains how the beautiful city came to be and what happened there when the Inca still reigned.

The Main Square

Cuzco is the center of the Inca empire and the main square is the center of Cuzco, so that's the obvious place to start your first tour of the city!

As you stand in the square and look at all the handsome stone buildings around you, it is difficult to realize that all the development you see is really quite new.

Until about 500 years ago, Cuzco was a large, rambling, rather ramshackle town on the edge of a misty swamp. According to tradition, things changed around 1440, in the reign of the emperor Pachacuti. He is believed to have decided to rebuild Cuzco. Certainly, the magnificent capital city you are about to explore is quite unlike that earlier town on the edge of the swamp, with all the damp, cold and diseases associated with such sites. Now Cuzco is a showplace for Inca craft skills, and a symbol of the Inca empire's power.

The reason for moving the city lay deep within the Incas' religious beliefs, which are difficult for visitors to learn about. But one of the reasons was the Incas' belief that Cuzco was the navel—the absolute center—of the whole world. All the empire's towns and villages were built within a series of magical (but invisible) lines. Building within these lines ensured good luck. There were, however, doubts about the position of Cuzco. So, after many sacrifices to the gods and long discussions with the senior priests, it was decided to move the city.

As a result, the center of the city was moved north, so that the main square in which you are now standing was at the center of all the empire's magical, invisible lines. Whether it was Pachacuti or another emperor who decided on the move does not really matter, the importance of Cuzco shows that the decision and choice of position were right—otherwise the empire would not have become so powerful.

The Inca name for the main square is Huacaypata. It is a vast open space covering about 10 acres (4 hectares), and is where many of the great religious ceremonies are staged. In the middle is a stone platform where the emperor stands to perform his ritual duties.

If you are lucky enough to be visiting Cuzco on the first day of the month you'll find the square packed with people, because a special ceremony is taking place. The emperor and his courtiers have come to inspect 100 specially chosen llamas and then to watch them being led four times in a circle around images of the most important gods. The high priest then dedicates the llamas to Viracocha and shares them out among 30 high-ranking government officials. Each receives three or four llamas.

After the ceremony is over, wait for the crowds to clear before starting your exploration of the city. As you wait, have a look at the halls and palaces around the square. No one will mind if you pause to look at them, but take care not to linger too long—it might cause suspicious glances in your direction.

Discussion Questions

1. **How does a "guided tour" of the ancient city of Cuzco help you understand more about the Inca?**
2. **What parts of the tour help you understand the importance of religion to the Inca?**

from

The Essential Codex Mendoza

by Frances F. Berdan and Patricia Rieff Anawalt

Folio 2r (shown on p. 71 of the pupil edition) is a page of the *Codex Mendoza.* This folio shows the founding of Tenochtitlan, the capital of the Aztec empire. A prophecy said that the Aztecs would find their home in a lake that held the heart of their god's enemy. According to the prophecy, a cactus would grow from a rock where the heart had fallen, and on the cactus would be an eagle. Have students look at the illustration on page 71 of their pupil edition while you read.

The Island Section of Folio 2r

glyph: symbol that gives information

The Eagle on the Cactus

The most dominant image of folio 2r is the eagle perched atop a prickly pear cactus that grows from the Aztec glyph for rock. This same symbol appears in several other Colonial accounts, and still serves today—with the addition of a snake in the eagle's beak—as the national emblem of modern Mexico.

The eagle . . . is an Aztec symbol for the sun, which is associated with Huitzilopochtli, the Mexica's patron [god]. The cactus fruit the eagle is about to consume may represent the human hearts offered the sun to sustain it during the daily journey across the [sky].

The Shield and Arrows

Just as the eagle on the cactus symbolizes the founding of Tenochtitlan, the shield and arrows immediately below represent the city itself. A shield backed by arrows is an Aztec glyph for war. When the shield in question carries this particular design—the *ihuiteteyo* (down ball)—it represents the power of Tenochtitlan. . . .

Island Divided by Crossing Streams of Water

A goodly portion of folio 2r depicts a square divided "in the form of Saint Andrew's cross." This stylized plan represents the original small island in Lake Texcoco on which Tenochtitlan was founded, an islet divided in quarters by two waterways. It has been suggested that . . . this . . . differs from that of a modern map: north may not be at the top. . . .

speculation: guess
edifice: building
gloss: translation

The Division into Quadrants

. . . On folio 2r, two of the four divisions contain what could be construed as place-name glyphs. However, the Spanish commentary makes no mention of them, and to date no one has definitively determined what these images mean. The building in the upper quadrant has been variously identified as a *tecpan* (noble's house or government building), a *cabildo* or townhouse, and a temple of Huitzilopochtli. The [last] speculation is the most probable. The humble shrine that appears on folio 2r may well represent the first stage of what evolved into the magnificent sixteenth-century Templo Mayor. This was the towering one-hundred-foot-high edifice that so impressed Cortés and his men. . . .

The City's Founders

The four sections of the city all contain identically arrayed males. Each sits in the standard Aztec male posture, white *tilmatli* tightly wrapped about drawn-up legs. Nine of these figures, each seated on a bundle of green reeds, wear no body paint and have their hair arranged in the distinguished warrior hairstyle, the *temillotl* (pillar of stone). The tenth and largest of these dignitaries is seated on a yellow woven mat in the left quadrant. His black body paint, smear of blood at the temple, and loosely tied-back hair signify that he is a priest. Only this male, whose glyph and Spanish gloss indicate that he was named Tenuch, has a speech glyph. As the Spanish commentary confirms, he is the leader of the group. . . .

The nine dignitaries who surround Tenuch also are identified by both name glyph and Spanish gloss. The three figures seated behind Tenuch have glosses reading Xocoyol ("Foot Bell"), Teçineuh ("He Who Expels Someone"), and Oçelopan ("Jaguar Banner"). The latter's gloss is misplaced, as his name glyph indicates. This male is really Acaçitli ("Reed Hare"); Oçelopan, complete with his ocelot-banner name glyph, is the left-hand figure in the upper quadrant. Facing him is Quapan ("Eagle Banner"). In the right-hand quadrant sits Aguexotl ("Water Willow") and Xomimitl ("Foot Arrow"). The lower quadrant contains Atototl ("Water Bird") and Xiuhcaqui ("Person Shod with Turquoise-Colored Sandals"). Along with Tenuch, these nine dignitaries apparently were the founders of Tenochtitlan.

Discussion Questions

1. **Do you think this page presents factual information? Explain your answer.**
2. **Do you think this was a good way to record history? Why or why not?**

from

The Iroquois Constitution

The Iroquois League was—and still is—a united group of Native American tribes led by one chief and 50 representatives from the tribes. At the time the league was formed, around 1580, its five tribes were 12,000 strong. This is an excerpt from their constitution.

confederate: united for a common purpose

disposition: nature, character

1. I am Dekanawidah and with the Five Nations' Confederate Lords I plant the Tree of Great Peace. I plant it in your territory, Adodarhoh, and the Onondaga Nation, in the territory of you who are Firekeepers.

I name the tree the Tree of the Great Long Leaves. Under the shade of this Tree of the Great Peace we spread the soft white feathery down of the globe thistle as seats for you, Adodarhoh, and your cousin Lords.

We place you upon the seats, spread soft with the feathery down of the globe thistle, there beneath the shade of the spreading branches of the Tree of Peace. . . .

2. Roots have spread out from the Tree of the Great Peace, one to the north, one to the east, one to the south and one to the west. The name of these roots is The Great White Roots and their nature is Peace and Strength.

If any man or any nation outside the Five Nations shall obey the laws of the Great Peace and make known their disposition to the Lords of the Confederacy, they may trace the Roots to the Tree and if their minds are clean and they are obedient and promise to obey the wishes of the Confederate Council, they shall be welcomed to take shelter beneath the Tree of the Long Leaves.

We place at the top of the Tree of the Long Leaves an Eagle who is able to see afar.

If he sees in the distance any evil approaching or any danger threatening he will at once warn the people of the Confederacy.

Discussion Questions

1. **Why do you think the Iroquois chose a tree as a symbol for peace within the league?**
2. **In what ways might the five tribes have needed each other's help after the arrival of Europeans?**

from

My Indian Boyhood

by Chief Luther Standing Bear

Chief Standing Bear lived from around 1868 until 1939. His memoir of his childhood, dedicated to "the boys and girls of America," was published in 1931. He wrote this book, he said, so that white children would better understand Sioux children.

My parents belonged to that great plains tribe which is now called the Sioux. But before the white man came, we called ourselves the Lakotas. The first white men to come to this country thought they had discovered India, a land they had been searching for, so they named the people they found here Indians. Through the mistake of these first white settlers, we have been called Indians ever since.

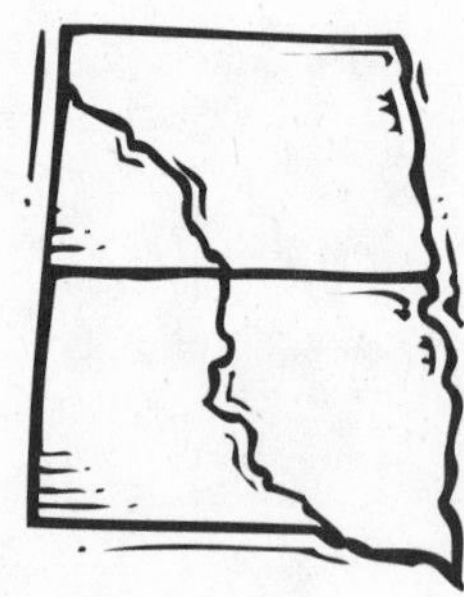

Now the big Missouri River runs through the country that my people inhabited. The part of the tribe that lived on the east side of the river called themselves Dakotas, and those who lived on the west side of this stream called themselves Lakotas. And I was born a Lakota.

Later, when many white people arrived in this country, they saw that my tribe was a very powerful and independent one. We kept our land to ourselves by making all other tribes stay away from us. Our warriors were brave and noted for their skill in fighting. Therefore, they were feared by all other tribes. The white people, seeing that we were feared by the tribes that surrounded us, began to fear us too, so they called us Sioux. The word "Sioux" is a French word and means "cutthroat." So that is how we became known as the Sioux. Some writers have called us the "Fighting Sioux"; others have called us the "Mighty Sioux." Our people were full of pride, but our women were quiet and gentle and our men were brave and dignified. We earned our right to pride, for it was a cardinal principle for the Sioux to be brave, and to be a coward was unforgivable. . . .

The home of my tribe, the Western Sioux, was all that territory which is now called North and South Dakota, and all this land once belonged to my people. It was a beautiful country. In the springtime and early summer the plains, as far as the eye could see, were covered with velvety green grass. Even the rolling hills were green, and here and there was a pretty stream. Over the hills roamed the buffalo and in the woods that bordered the streams were luscious fruits that were ours for the picking. In the winter everything was covered with snow, but we always had plenty of food to last through the winter until spring came again. . . .

A tipi was my first home. In it I was born, and my earliest recollection is playing around the fire and being watched over by my Indian mother. As a baby I swung in an Indian cradle from poles in the tipi. I was the first son of a chief and I was expected to grow up brave and fearless like my father. I was named Plenty Kill. My parents called me Ota K'te, for that was the way to say "Plenty Kill" in Sioux.

As I grew up, my father began to teach me all the things that a little Indian boy should know. When I was old enough to be put on a pony, he taught me to ride. He tied my pony to his with a rope and I rode this way until I had learned to handle the pony myself. When I had learned to ride, I went on short hunts with him and he taught me how to butcher small game. Finally, the eventful day came when I went on a buffalo hunt. That was an important day in my life when I went home to the tipi and told my mother I had killed a buffalo. She was proud of me and that made me happy.

I learned about the habits of wild animals and how to trap them. I learned to shoot birds with a bow and arrow and to roast them on the fire. I soon came to know much about the weather and how to prepare for the coming of winter by tanning skins for warm clothing. By knowing all these things, we had no fear of Nature, but on the contrary loved Nature. She seemed bountiful to us with all the things she had provided for our comfort.

At this time we lived close to Nature and knew nothing but Nature. We observed everything of the outdoors, and in this way learned many things that were good and helpful for us to know. The Indian knows that Nature is wise, and that by keeping our eyes open, we learn her wise ways.

Discussion Questions

1. Why would a Plains Indian child need a pony?

2. What is your opinion about living close to nature?

Students may want to find a library copy of *My Indian Boyhood* and read more of Chief Standing Bear's autobiography.

from

The Travels of Marco Polo

This is Marco Polo's account of his journey across Asia to China. In the first excerpt, he describes the palace of the grand khan. The second excerpt tells about the province of Tenduk.

constitute: make up
span: 9 inches
encompassing: including
balustrade: a railing held up by small posts
contrived: created
disposed: arranged
azure: blue
wrought: mad

Within these walls, which constitute the boundary of four miles, stands the palace of the grand khan, the most extensive that has ever yet been known. It reaches from the northern to the southern wall, leaving only a vacant space (or court), where persons of rank and the military guards pass and repass. It has no upper floor, but the roof is very lofty. The paved foundation or platform on which it stands is raised ten spans above the level of the ground, and a wall of marble, two paces wide, is built on all sides, to the level of this pavement, within the line of which the palace is erected; so that the wall, extending beyond the ground plan of the building, and encompassing the whole, serves as a terrace, where those who walk on it are visible from without. Along the exterior edge of the wall is a handsome balustrade, with pillars, which the people are allowed to approach. The sides of the great halls and the apartments are ornamented with dragons in carved work and gilt, figures of warriors, of birds, and of beasts, with representations of battles. The inside of the roof is contrived in such a manner that nothing besides gilding and painting presents itself to the eye. On each of the four sides of the palace there is a grand flight of marble steps, by which you ascend from the level of the ground to the wall of marble which surrounds the building, and which constitute the approach to the palace itself. The grand hall is extremely long and wide, and admits of dinners being there served to great multitudes of people. The palace contains a number of separate chambers, all highly beautiful, and so admirably disposed that it seems impossible to suggest any improvement to the system of their arrangement. The exterior of the roof is adorned with a variety of colors, red, green, azure, and violet, and the sort of covering is so strong as to last for many years. The glazing of the windows is so well wrought and so delicate as to have the transparency of crystal. In the rear of the body of the palace there are large buildings containing several apartments, where is deposited the private property of the monarch, or his treasure in gold and silver bullion, precious stones, and pearls, and also his vessels of gold and silver plate. . . .

CHAPTER LV: *Of the seat of government of the princes of the family of Prester John, called Gog and Magog—of the manners of its inhabitants—of their manufacture of silk—and of the mines of silver worked there.* In this province (of Tenduk) was the principal seat of government of the sovereigns styled Prester John, when they ruled over the Tartars of this and the neighboring countries, and which their successors occupy to the present hour. George, above-mentioned, is the fourth in descent from Prester John, of whose family he is regarded as the head. There are two regions in which they exercise dominion. These in our part of the world are named Gog and Magog, but by the natives Ung and Mongul; in each of which there is a distinct race of people. In Ung they are Gog, and in Mongul they are Tartars. Travelling seven days through this province, in an easterly direction, towards Cathay, you pass many towns inhabited by idolaters, as well as by Mahometans and Nestorian Christians. They gain their living by trade and manufactures, weaving, fine-gold tissues, ornamented with mother-of-pearl, named *nascici*, and silks of different textures and colours, not unlike those of Europe; together with a variety of woollen cloths. These people are all subjects of the grand khan. One of the towns, named Sindichin, is celebrated for the manufacture of all kinds of arms, and every article necessary for the equipment of troops. In the mountainous part of the province there is a place called Idifa, in which is a rich mine of silver, from whence large quantities of that metal are obtained. There are also plenty of birds and beasts.

idolaters: those who worship idols

Nestorian Christians: followers of a Christian doctrine that said Jesus Christ was two persons, one human and one divine

Discussion Questions

1. **How do you think Marco Polo and his father and uncle felt as they entered the palace of Kubiai Khan? What makes you think so?**
2. **Why do you think Marco Polo uses great detail to describe what he sees?**

from

When China Ruled the Seas

by Louise Levathes

This is a poem inscribed on a tablet erected by Zheng He in Malacca, in what is now Malaysia.

Middle Kingdom: Chinese name for the Chinese Empire

luxuriate: rest in luxury

suzerainty: power of a feudal lord

demeanor: outward behavior

enfeoffed: invested by law

posterity: future generations

The vast southwestern sea reaches unto the Middle Kingdom,
its waves cresting high as the heavens,
watering the earth, the same way for countless eons.
Washed by sunlight, bathed in the moonlight,
its luminous seascape is harmonious. Rain-swept crags
and dewy rocks in its midst luxuriate with vegetation.
Golden ornaments and precious filigrees [from these lands]
are resplendent with reds and blues.
And in such a place people live in harmony.
Its righteous king, paying his respects to imperial
suzerainty, wishes his country to be treated as one of
our imperial domains and to follow the Chinese way.
He comes and goes in the midst of a retinue, rows of
parasols unfurled around him. In performing rituals,
his demeanor and dress are pious and reverent.
So here writ large on everlasting stone we do proclaim
your loyalty; your country's western mountain shall
forever be enfeoffed as a Guardian Peak.
The lords of the mountains and earls of the seas
shall all join its retinue, when the spirit of
our deceased imperial father descends from on high.
Posterity will smile upon your deed as time passes;
and your sons and grandsons will have
limitless good fortune.

Discussion Questions

1. **Why do you think the king of Malacca wanted his country to become part of the Chinese empire and "follow the Chinese way"?**
2. **Why do you think Zheng He erected a tablet in Malacca?**

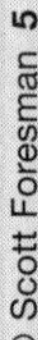

from

al-Bakri and Ibn Battuta

The first of these selections was written by al-Bakri, an 11th-century Arab writer who lived in Spain. It describes the court of Tunka Manin in the kingdom of Ghana. The second, written by Ibn Battuta, a 14th-century Muslim scholar, describes the court of Mansa Suleyman, Mansa Musa's successor in the kingdom of Mali.

When [the king] gives an audience to his people, to listen to their complaints and set them to rights, he sits in a pavilion around which stand his horses caparisoned in cloth of gold; behind him stand ten pages holding shields and gold-mounted swords; and on his right are the sons of the princes of his empire, splendidly clad and with gold plaited into their hair. The governor of the city is seated on the ground next to the king, and all around him are his counsellors in the same position. The gate of the chamber is guarded by dogs of an excellent breed. These dogs never leave the king's seat. They wear collars of gold and silver, ornamented with metals.

caparisoned: outfitted

ebony: hard, heavy, dark wood

The lord of this kingdom has a great balcony in his palace. There he has a great seat of ebony that is like a throne fit for a large and tall person. It is flanked by elephants' tusks. The king's arms stand near him. They are all of gold; sword and lance, bow and quiver of arrows. . . . Before him stand about twenty Turkish or other pages, who are brought from Cairo. One of these, standing on his left, holds a silk umbrella that is topped by a dome and bird of gold. The bird is like a hawk. The king's officers are seated in a circle near him, in two rows, one to the right and one to the left. Beyond them sit the commanders of the cavalry. In front of him there is a person who never leaves him and who is his executioner; and another who is his official spokesman, and who is named the herald. In front of him there are also drummers. Others dance before their king and make him merry.

Discussion Questions

1. **Why do you think the kings wanted to present a powerful image to traders?**
2. **How do you think trading between nations or kingdoms can bring about changes in customs, language, religion?**

To the Edge of the World!

by Rachel Wright

This article from a fictional newspaper, *The Viking News,* tells the story of Viking father and son, Erik the Red and Leif Erikson, and how each discovered and settled land west of Iceland where no European had been before.

Between the years 982 and 1001, a Viking father and son both explored farther west than any European had ever dared. And by discovering two new lands, they astonished the Viking world.

Viking explorers need to be tough, and no one was tougher than Erik the Red. His great voyages began in 982, when he was exiled from Iceland for three years for killing two men in a feud.

Erik promptly picked a crew and went to sea in search of an unexplored land that was rumored to lie west of Iceland.

A World of Ice and Snow

Erik and his crew sailed the Atlantic Ocean until at last they saw the land they sought. Its east coast was entirely icebound and uninviting, so they sailed on along the coast. And there, on the southwest shores, they found ice-free land with plenty of good green pastures.

Three years later, Erik came back to Iceland, bursting with tales about the marvelous place he called Greenland.

By that time, Iceland was becoming crowded, and farmland was scarce, so Erik's stories appealed to many. In 986, some 25 ships left for Greenland under Erik's command.

It was a dangerous voyage, and only 14 ships made it safely to the new land. But two settlements were founded that have flourished ever since.

But that wasn't the end of the explorations. In the same year, a man named Bjarni Herjolfsson sighted a new landmass, which was even farther west than Greenland.

No one was more excited by Bjarni's story than Erik's son, Leif. And, determined to match his father's achievement, Leif set out in 1000 in search of the mysterious land.

Leif Eriksson sailed west until he reached a rocky, barren shore. He then headed south, past a forested coast, until he found a land that was richly fertile.

When he returned to Greenland in 1001, Leif described his discovery to *The Viking News* and explained why he had called the land Vinland.

"There were lots of vines, laden with berries called grapes," he said. "I hadn't seen wild grapes before, but one of my slaves is from Germany, where grapes grow, and he knew what they were."

Leif's expedition was soon followed by others, all eager to bring home Vinland's vast supplies of timber, grapes, and fur.

Some hardy folk also tried to settle in Vinland, but it proved to be one Viking colony too many.

What Leif didn't know when he found Vinland was that people were already living there. Soon, fights between locals and settlers grew so fierce that the Vikings had to leave.

A Place Too Far From Home

One dejected settler told *The Viking News* that the colony could never have survived. "It's too far from Greenland," she said, "and far from essential supplies of tools and weapons."

Despite this setback, however, *The Viking News* salutes the achievements of Erik and Leif. Between them, they have unlocked the mysteries of the far western seas and the unknown lands beyond.

And in so doing, they have proved again that we Vikings are the greatest explorers in the western world!

Discussion Questions

1. **Why do you think the author presented this information in the form of an imaginary news article?**
2. **What character traits do you think led Erik the Red to explore and settle in Greenland?**
3. **What might have made the Vinland settlement a success?**

Students might enjoy writing their own imaginary news article about some historical event that interests them.

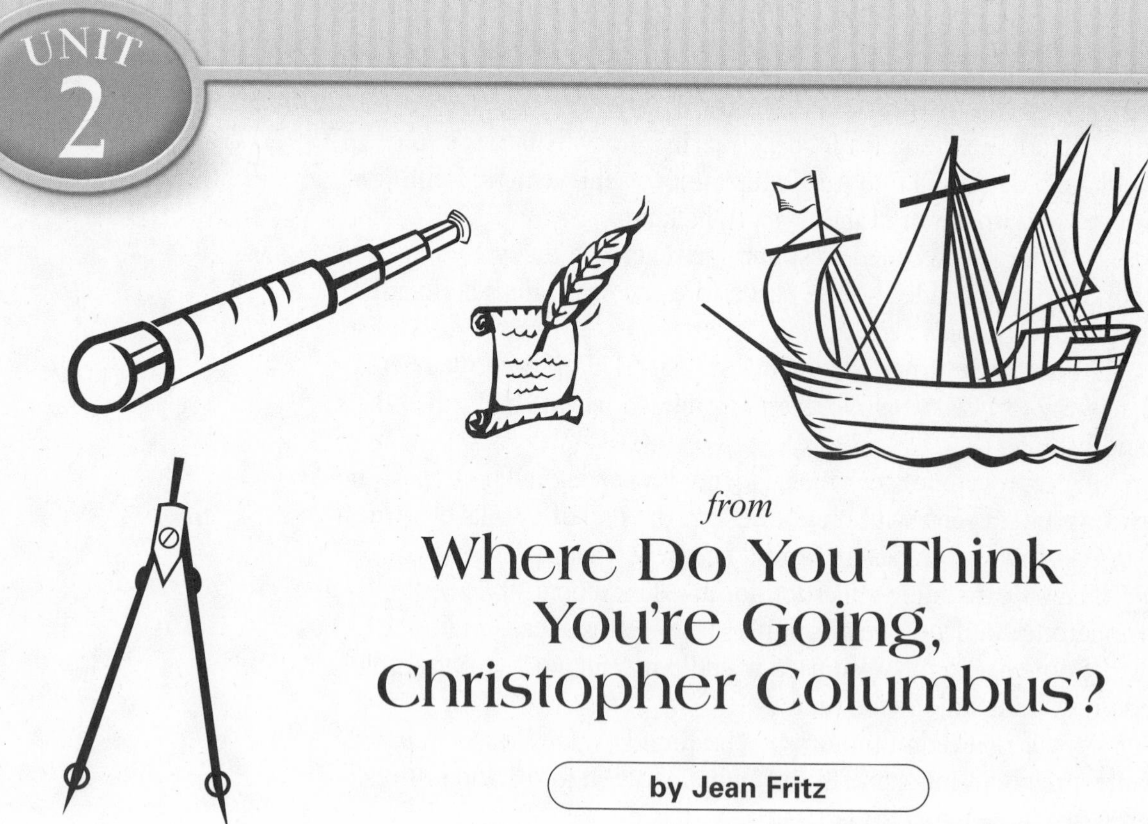

from

Where Do You Think You're Going, Christopher Columbus?

by Jean Fritz

This excerpt from Jean Fritz's biography of Columbus tells about the end of his exploring days, when he had given up finding a route to India.

Hispaniola: island between Cuba and Puerto Rico

King Solomon: king of Israel

malaria: a disease spread via mosquito

Gold. That was what he was after now. North of Panama was a land where he'd found more signs of gold than he'd found in four years in Hispaniola. Indeed, it was here, he said, that King Solomon of Biblical times must have had his gold mines. Columbus spent the spring in this country, building a fort to serve as a trading post, but right from the beginning, the natives had been suspicious and unfriendly. They had a strange custom of turning their backs when they spoke, which, of course, made sign language difficult. But it was clear that they didn't care to talk. On April 6, 1503, a force of 400 natives attacked the Spanish fort and before the fighting was over, twelve Spaniards had been killed.

Columbus, sick with malaria and running a high fever, had been left alone on shipboard. He could hear the battle, but when he cried out to his captains, there was no reply. He must have fainted, he reported later, and while unconscious, he seemed to hear a voice telling him not to be discouraged. Yes, he was an old man, the voice said, but he would still perform brave deeds. Good things still lay in store for him.

This was a comfort to Columbus, but obviously no brave deeds were in order right then. What he and his men had to do now was to escape. Abandoning the fort, King Solomon's mine, and one ship stuck on a sandbar, Columbus set sail for Hispaniola, not even sure he could make it there. His ships had been so eaten by shipworms that they were falling apart, and, indeed, another ship had to be abandoned within a few days. For two months the two remaining ships stumbled through the water while the men pumped and bailed, but on June 25, when they reached the island of Jamaica, the ships could stay afloat no longer. The men ran them ashore and beached them close together, for this was where they would live. For how long, no one knew. They were marooned.

marooned: put ashore in an isolated place

mutinied: rebelled against a ship's officers

Columbus was stranded on Jamaica for one year and five days. He spent most of that time trying to control his men (half of them mutinied), trying to keep peace with the natives (who supplied them with food), and feeling sorry for himself.

At first he had hoped for a quick rescue. Diego Mendez, a gentleman volunteer, had left in a native canoe in July for Hispaniola to bring help. But as summer turned into winter and winter into spring, Columbus decided that Diego had drowned on the way. What else could he think? He had no way of knowing that Diego had reached Hispaniola safely but that the governor was in no hurry to help Christopher Columbus. He had no ship large enough that he could spare, he said, nor did he send one until June 1504.

Columbus was fifty-three years old now, in poor health, and impatient to see the queen. He still had brave deeds to perform, he wanted to tell her. But there were delays in Hispaniola. There was bad weather at sea. Columbus did not reach Spain until November 7, 1504. And he never did see Queen Isabella. She died on November 26, three weeks after his arrival.

Discussion Questions

1. **Why was Columbus so interested in the signs of gold north of Panama?**
2. **How would you describe Columbus's character during these last years of exploring?**

Students may want to read the entire book, *Where Do You Think You're Going, Christopher Columbus?*, or look in a library for Columbus's own journal of his voyages.

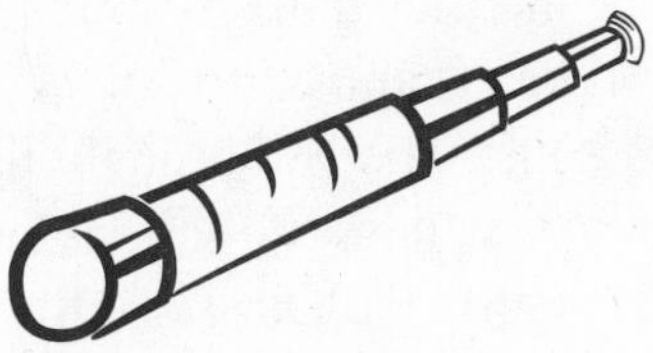

from

Castaways

by Alvar Núñez Cabeza de Vaca

In 1542, Cabeza de Vaca published an account of his journey overland from the Texas Gulf Coast through the Southwest to Culiacán near the Pacific coast of present-day Mexico. These excerpts from his account describe a search for maize and the villages and people the group encountered.

maize: corn

Southern Sea: Pacific Ocean

reed: stem of a tall, slender grass that grows in marshy land

league: about 3 miles

How We Followed the Maize Road

After we had been there for two days we determined to go and look for maize and did not want to follow the path of the cattle because it was toward the north, and this was very much out of our way, for we were always sure that by going toward the setting sun we would find what we desired: and so we continued on our way and crossed the whole country until we came to the Southern Sea, and the fear that the Indians tried to instill in us of the great hunger we would have to endure (as indeed we did endure) was not sufficient to deter us for all of the seventeen days of the journey they had told us of. During all those days, as we traveled up the river, they gave us many cattle hides, and we did not eat that fruit of theirs, but each day our rations were a handful of deer fat that we tried always to keep on hand for these emergencies. And so we passed all the seventeen days and at the end of them we crossed the river and traveled for another seventeen, in the direction of the sunset, through plains and between the very high mountains that are there; we found some people there who eat nothing but powdered straw for the third part of the year, and because when we passed through it was that time of year, we also had to eat it until those days of journeying ended, when we found permanent houses where much maize was stored, and they gave us a great quantity of it and its flour, and squash and beans and cotton blankets, and we loaded everything onto those people who had brought us there, who with all these supplies returned the happiest folk in the world.

We gave many thanks to God Our Lord for bringing us there, where we found so much food. Among these houses were some made of earth, and all the others are made of reed mats; and from there we went on for a hundred leagues and always found permanent houses and good supplies of maize and beans. And they gave us many deer and many cotton blankets, better than those of

New Spain. They also gave us many beads and some corals that are found in the Southern Sea and many very fine turquoises that they have, which come from the north; and in a word, the people here gave us everything they had, and they gave me five emeralds made into arrow points, and with these arrows they perform their rites and dances. And, as it seemed to me that they were very good, I asked them where they had procured them, and they said that they were brought from some very high mountains that are toward the north, and that they bought them in exchange for plumes and parrot feathers; and they said that there were towns there with many people and very large houses. . . .

rite: formal act or ceremony

procure: get

How They Gave Us Hearts of Deer

In the village where they gave us the emeralds, they gave Dorantes more than six hundred hearts of deer, opened, of which they always have a great abundance for their food; and so we called it the Village of the Hearts, and it is the gateway to many provinces that are on the Southern Sea; and if those who go to look for the sea do not pass through here they will be lost, for there is no maize on the coast and they eat powdered herbs and straw, and fish that they take in the sea with rafts, for they are too primitive to have canoes. . . . We believe that near the coast, along the route of those villages that we found, are more than a thousand leagues of populated country and good supplies of food, for the people sow beans and maize three times a year. There are three kinds of deer, and those of one kind are as large as yearling bulls in Castile. . . .

We stayed in this village three days, and a day's journey from there was another village in which we were caught in such a rainstorm that, because a river rose very high, we could not cross and stayed for fifteen days. During this time Castillo saw a buckle from a sword belt hanging around the neck of an Indian, with a horseshoe nail sewed to it; he took it from him and we asked him what that was, and the Indians told us that it had come from heaven. We asked further, who had brought it from there? and they replied that those who brought it were some men who wore beards like us, and who had come from heaven and reached that river, and that they had horses and lances and swords, and that they had wounded two of their people with lances.

Discussion Questions

1. **What skills and abilities helped Cabeza de Vaca and his men survive?**
2. **Why do you think Cabeza de Vaca's men wanted to know more about the other bearded men?**

from

The Generall Historie of Virginia, New England, and the Summer Isles

by John Smith

In his writings about Jamestown, John Smith praised its soil and resources, perhaps hoping to convince new settlers to come from England. This passage describes the area around the colony.

millstones: large, flat, round stones used to grind grain

crystal: transparent quartz

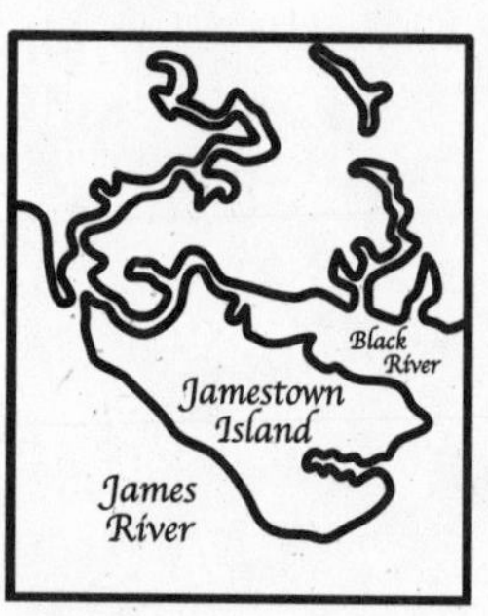

There is but one entrance by sea into this country, and that is at the mouth of a very goodly bay, 18 or 20 miles broad. The cape on the south is called Cape Henry, in honor of our most noble Prince. The land, white hilly sands like unto the Downs, and all along the shores great plenty of pines and firs.

The north cape is called Cape Charles, in honor of the worthy Duke of York. The isles before it, Smith's Isles, by the name of the discover[er].

Within is a country that may have the prerogative [natural advantage] over the most pleasant places known, for large and pleasant navigable rivers, heaven and earth never agreed better to frame a place for man's habitation; were it fully manured [cultivated] and inhabited by industrious people. Here are mountains, hills, plains, valleys, rivers, brooks, all running most pleasantly into a fair bay, compassed but for the mouth, with fruitful and delightsome land. In the bay and rivers are many isles both great and small, some woody, some plain, most of them low and not inhabited. This bay lieth north and south, in which the water floweth near 200 miles, and hath a channel for 140 miles, of depth betwixt 6 and 15 fathoms, holding in breadth for the most part 10 or 14 miles. From the head of the bay to the northwest, the land is mountainous, and so in a manner from thence by a southwest line; so that the more southward, the farther off from the bay are those mountains. From which fall certain brooks which after come to five principal navigable rivers. These run from the northwest into the southeast, and so into the west side of the bay, where the fall [mouth] of every river is within 20 or 15 miles one of another.

The mountains are of divers natures: for at the head of the bay the rocks are of a composition like millstones. Some of marble, &c. And many pieces like crystal we found, as thrown down by water from these mountains. For in winter they are covered with much snow, and when it dissolveth the waters fall with such violence, that it causeth great inundations in some narrow valleys, which is scarce[ly] perceived being once in the rivers. These waters wash from the rocks such glistering tinctures, that the ground in some places seemeth as gilded, where both the rocks and the earth are so splendent to behold, that better judgments than ours might have been persuaded, they contained more than probabilities.

The vesture [vegetation] of the earth in most places doth manifestly prove the nature of the soil to be lusty and very rich. . . . Generally for the most part it is a black, sandy mold, in some places a fat, slimy clay, in other places a very barren gravel. But the best ground is known by the vesture it beareth, as by the greatness of trees, or abundance of weeds, &c.

The country is not mountainous, nor yet low, but such pleasant plain hills, and fertile valleys, one prettily crossing another, and watered so conveniently with fresh brooks and springs, no less commodious than delightsome. By the rivers are many plain marshes, containing some 20, some 100, some 200 acres, some more, some less. Other plains there are few, but only where the savages inhabit: but all [is] overgrown with trees and weeds, being a plain wilderness as God first made it.

inundations: floods
glistering tinctures: shining dyes
gilded: coated with gold
splendent: shining
commodious: roomy

Discussion Questions

1. **What kind of picture of this new land does Smith present?**
2. **If you had lived in John Smith's time and read this description, would you have been interested in joining the colony? Why or why not?**

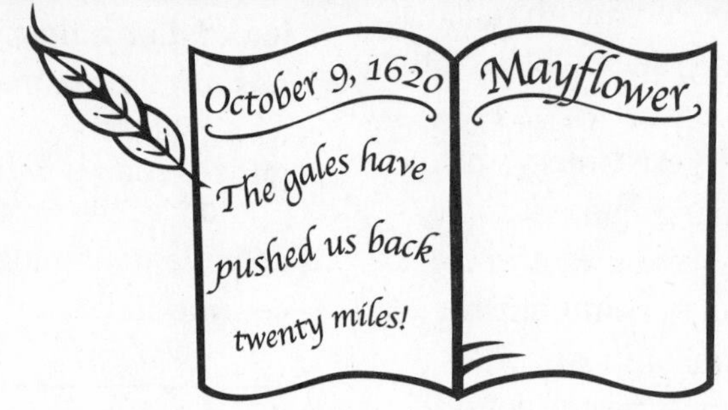

from

A Journey to the New World

by Kathryn Lasky

The following excerpts are entries in the fictional journal of a 12-year-old English girl on the *Mayflower,* based on historical descriptions of the 1620 passage from England to America.

breadth: width
plodding: slow
Pope: head of the Roman Catholic church

October 1, 1620. Morning
Mayflower
1150 miles sailed

"Mem," that's what I answer to. 'Tis short for Remember. My full name being Remember Patience Whipple. Patience was to be my first name, but Mam, my mother, decided it was wrong. I was squally and impatient. They wanted, however, to remember my mother's dear sister who had just passed on. So they slipped the Patience in-between. For some it is a good first name, for me it is better as an in-between name. Mam says I am more patient than I once was, but I still have a far way to go. I'm twelve years old. Maybe by the time I am full grown, say fifteen, I shall be patient.

We are journeying to the New World. It is the *Mayflower* that be getting us there, slowly. She measures ninety feet in length and twenty-five feet in breadth at her broadest point. She is a strong ship but a plodding one, as she creaks her way across this vast gray Atlantic sea.

The reason for our journey is our religion. You see, we are not the Pope's people nor the King's really, but God's people. We are Saints of the Holy Discipline. "Saints"—for short. That is what all of us English who went to Holland are called. And if we go to this New World, free from old King James and all the fancy church rituals that are not to our way, we can worship as we want. You see, we believe that the church is in our heart and not in a building. So 'tis our hearts that lead us. . . .

October 2, 1620
Mayflower

Storm-force winds; too dangerous to go topside to seek out Master Jones for our progress. 'Tis hard to imagine what this New World shall be like. I am used to towns with buildings and winding streets. And people bustling to market and talking Dutch, or English if they be one of us. But the New World is empty of all that. There are no buildings or streets and the only people are feathered men and feathered women and feathered babies, I suppose, who do paint their faces 'tis said, and live in most uncommon shelters.

topside: on a boat's deck

gale: very strong wind

October 2, 1620. Afternoon
Mayflower

They say we be heading for northern Virginia, near the Hudson River. The King, King James of England, granted the land. Then the merchants formed the company for a plantation where we shall grow things to send back to England to sell.

Too sick to write. . . .

October 4, 1620
Mayflower
1300 miles sailed

Will Butten, Deacon Fuller's servant, is a clever lad. All the littlest children were carrying on something fierce. Wailing as loud as the storm. He took a pen nib and painted faces on his fingers and then again where his thumb joins his hand. Each face had a name and then he began to tell a story by wiggling his fingers. Soon they all stopped crying. Hummy, my friend, and I think he is quite dear. . . .

October 9, 1620
Mayflower

The gales have pushed us back twenty miles! We are practically back to where we were yesterday! I am most depressed. This wind is indeed like a big fist in our face. Father says the ship cannot go against it when the wind be square on! Agony!

October 10, 1620
Mayflower
1560 miles sailed

I write now with trembling hand. A most horrendous thing has happened. There was what they call a rogue wave that rose out of the storm seas. It felt as if our poor little ship was flying for endless seconds and then there was a terrible crack. Yes, indeed we have cracked the main beam! It surely buckled and now the deck above us is like a sieve and we are all drenched. All the men came together. All so grim-faced. And then 'twas my own father who perhaps has solved the problem, for he remembered the immense iron screw we brought from Holland for building our village in the New World. . . . I must have faith in God and man. These men, my father, the carpenter, the sailing master, Master Bradford, Elder Brewster, they will figure out something. We all pray that 'tis possible to raise the broken beam back into place and then with a post under it, secure it once it is mended.

October 12, 1620
Mayflower
1790 miles sailed

It has worked. God's providence has come down on our little ship. The main beam is raised and repaired! We are blessed. Last evening we assembled for prayers of thanks. Soon after that the winds abated and the rigging became quiet for the first time in nearly two weeks. We could hear to think, hear to pray, hear to listen to each other. And Hummy and I chattered all through the night. . . .

October 13, 1620
Mayflower
1805 miles sailed

Last evening Mam was able to cook over the charcoal brazier for the first time in days. We had a nice supper. It was a flesh day so we could have meat. We did, salt beef with mustard and vinegar, peas, ship biscuit, and Blessing had her favorite: warmed-up oatmeal. I would love a bag pudding or some Frumenty, the kind Mam makes all thick and full of cinnamon. It drips off your spoon so nice and warm. But that we shall have to wait a long time for.

In any case, it is a fine day now. The gray skies have washed away leaving this immense blue bowl over our heads. We have fresh, steady winds, northeasterlies. The monkeys, as they call the sailors who scramble up the masts, were in the rigging and every piece of canvas has been shaken out. *Mayflower* looks like a many-winged bird with her fore and main courses flying, and the topsails swelling against the sky!

We are allowed topside and I do not feel sick anymore, not one speck of the quissies. We set ourselves in earnest now for the New World!! And not only is the ship's course set, but I feel that I, too, can begin in earnest with my diary. I have a name for you now. But first you must know your history—how you came to be. I shall write that down tomorrow. For now I want to enjoy the fresh breezes.

Discussion Questions

1. **Does the diary seem realistic to you? Why or why not?**
2. **What would have been the hardest part of the journey for you, if you had been on board the *Mayflower?***

A Letter from

Edward Winslow

Edward Winslow's letter of December 11, 1621, gives news of the settlers' first harvest, friendship with the Native American neighbors, and advice to future colonists from England for both the voyage to and homemaking in Plymouth.

Loving, and old Friend, although I received no Letter from you by this Ship, yet forasmuch as I know you expect the performance of my promise, which was, to write unto you truely and faithfully of all things. I have therefore at this time sent unto you accordingly. Referring you for further satisfaction to our more large Relations. You shall understand, that in this little time, that a few of us have beene here, we have built seaven dwelling houses, and foure for the use of the Plantation, and have made preparation for divers others. We set the last Spring some twentie Acres of Indian Corne, and sowed some six Acres of Barly & Pease, and according to the manner of the Indians, we manured our ground with Herings or rather Shadds, which we have in great abundance, and rake with great ease at our doores Our Corne did prove well, & God be praysed, we had a good increase of Indian Corne, and our Barly indifferent good, but our Pease not worth the gathering, for we feared they were too late sowne, they came up very well and blossomed, but the Sunne parched them in the blossome; our harvest being gotten in, our Governour sent foure men on fowling, that so we might after a more speciall manner rejoyce together, after we had gathered the fruit of our labours; they foure in one day killed as much fowle, as with a little helpe beside, served the Company almost a weeke, at which time amongst other Recreations, we exercised our Armes, many of the Indians coming amongst us, and amongst the rest their greatest King Massasoyt, with some nintie men, whom for three dayes we entertained and feasted. And they went out and killed five Deere, which they brought to the Plantation and bestowed on our Governour, and upon the Captaine, and others. And although it be not alwayes so plentifull, as it was at this time with us, yet by the goodnesse of God, we are so farre from want, that we often wish you partakers of our plentie. Wee have found the Indians very faithfull in their Covenant of Peace with us; very loving and readie to pleasure us; we often goe to them, and they come to us; some of us have bin fiftie myles by Land in the Country

yet forasmuch as I know: as far as I know

fowling: bird hunting

Massasoyt: Massasoit

Plantation: a colony or new settlement

possess the Indians with: give to the Indians

made sute unto us: made requests, followed

soveraigne: ruler

Kine: cattle

sallet: salad

Damsen: small, purple plum

with them; the occasions and Relations whereof you shall understand by our generall and more full Declaration of such things as are worth the noting, yea, it hath pleased God so to possesse the Indians with a feare of us, and love unto us, that not onely the greatest King amongst them called Massasoyt, but also all the Princes and peoples round about us, have either made sute unto us, or beene glad of any occasion to make peace with us, so that seaven of them at once have sent their messengers to us to that end, yea, an Fle at sea which we never saw hath also together with the former yielded willingly to be under the protection, and subjects to our soveraigne Lord King James, so that there is now great peace amongst the Indians themselves, which was not formerly, neither would have bin but for us; and we for our parts walke as peaceably and safely in the wood, as in the hie wayes in England, we entertaine them familiarly in our houses, and they as friendly bestowing their Venison on us. They are a people without any Religion, or knowledge of any God, yet very trustie, quicke of apprehension, ripe witted, just; . . . the temper of the ayre, here it agreeth well with that in England, and if there be any difference at all, this is somewhat hotter in Summer, some thinke it to be colder in Winter, but I cannot out of experience so say; the ayre is very cleere and not foggie, as hath beene reported. I never in my life remember a more seasonable yeare, then we have here enjoyed: and if we have once but Kine, Horses, and Sheepe, I make no question, but men might live as contented here as in any part of the world. For fish and fowle, we have great abundance, fresh Codd in the Summer is but course meat with us, our Bay is full of Lobsters all the Summer, and affordeth varietie of other Fish; in September we can take a Hogshead of Eeles in a night, with small labour, & can dig them out of their beds, all the Winter we have Mussells and Othus at our doores. Oysters we have none neere, but we can have them brought by the Indians when we will; all the Spring time the earth sendeth forth naturally very good Sallet Herbs: here are Grapes, white and red, and very sweete and strong also. Strawberies, Gooseberies, Raspas, &c. Plums of three sorts, with blacke and red, being almost as good as a Damsen: abundance of Roses, white, red, and damask: single, but very sweet indeed; the Countrey wanteth onely industrious men to imploy, for it would grieve your hearts (if as I) you had seene so many myles together by goodly Rivers uninhabited, and withall to consider those parts of the world wherein you live, to be even greatly burthened with abundance of people. These things I thought good to let you understand, being the truth of things as nere as I could experimentally take knowledge of, and that you might on our behalfe give God thankes who hath delt so favourably with us.

Our supply of men from you came the ninth of November 1621. putting in at Cape Cod, some eight or ten leagues from us, the Indians that dwell thereabout were they who were owners of the Corne which we found in Caves, for which we have given them full content, and are in great league with them, they sent us word there was a ship nere unto them, but thought it to be a French man, and indeede for our selves, we expected not a friend so soone. But when we perceived that she made for our Bay, the Governor commanded a great Peece to be shot off, to call home such as were abroad at worke; whereupon every man, yea, boy that could handle a Gun were readie, with full resolution, that if she were an Enemy, we would stand in our just defense, not fearing them, but God provided better for us then we supposed; these came all in health unto us, not any being sicke by the way (otherwise then by Sea sicknesse) and so continue at this time, by the blessing of God, the good wife Ford was delivered of a sonne the first night shee landed, and both of them are very well. When it pleaseth God, we are settled and fitted for the fishing business, and other trading, I doubt not but by the blessing of God, the gayne will give content to all; in the meane time, that we have gotten we have sent by this ship, and though it be not much, yet it will witnesse for us, that we have not beene idle, considering the smallnesse of our number all this Summer. We hope the Marchants will accept of it, and be incouraged to furnish us with things needfull for further imployment, which will also incourage us to put forth our selves to the uttermost. Now because I expect your comming unto us with other of our friends, whose companie we much desire, I thought good to advertise you of a few things needfull; be careful to have a very good bread-roome to put your Biskets in, let your Cask for . . . Water be Iron-bound for the first tyre if not more; let not your meat be drie salted, none can better doe it then the Saylers; let your meale be so hard trodd in your Cask that you shall need an Ads or Hatchet to worke it out with: Trust not too much on us for Corne at this time, for by reason of this last company that came, depending wholly upon us, we shall have little enough till harvest; be careful to come by some of your meale to spend by the way, it will much refresh you, build your Cabbins as open as you can, and bring good store of clothes, and bedding with you; bring every man a Musket or fowling Peece, let your Peece be long in the barrel, and feare not the waight of it, for most of our shooting is from Stands; bring juyce of Lemons, and take it fasting, it is of good use; for hot waters, Anni-seed water is the best, but use it sparingly: if you bring any thing for comfort in the Country, Butter or Sallet oyle, or both is very good; our Indian Corne even the coursest, maketh as pleasant meat as Rice, therefore spare that unlesse to spend by the way; bring Paper, and Linced oyle for your Windowes, with Cotton yarne for your Lamps; let your shotte be

league: 3 miles

Peece: gun

advertise you: inform you

Saylers: sailors

Anni-seed water: anise seed water

linced oyle: linseed oil

most for bigge Fowles, and bring store of Powder and shot: I forbeare further to write for the present, hoping to see you by the next returne, so I take my leave, commending you to the Lord for a safe conduct into us. Resting in him

Plimmouth in New England
This 11 of December.
1621.
Your loving Friend
E.W.

Discussion Questions

1. **What are some reasons why Edward Winslow might have written this letter?**
2. **Why do you think Winslow says that industrious people should come to the settlement?**
3. **Why might merchants in England be willing to send supplies to Plimoth Plantation?**

A Letter from

John Winthrop to Margaret Winthrop

The letter excerpted below was written by the Puritan leader of the Massachusetts Bay Colony, John Winthrop. In it, he discusses practical matters related to physical survival in his colony and tells his wife tells what he needs her to bring from England.

July 23, 1630
My dear wife:

. . . Be sure to be warm clothed and to have store of fresh provisions: meal, eggs put up in salt or ground malt, butter, oatmeal, peas, and fruits, and a large, strong chest or two, well locked, to keep these provisions in, and be sure they be bestowed in the ship where they may be readily come by, which the boatswain will see to and the quartermasters, if they be rewarded beforehand. But for these things my son will take care. Be sure to have ready at sea two or three skillets of several sizes, a large frying pan, a small stewing pan, and a case to boil a pudding in, store of linen for use at sea, . . . some drinking vessels, and pewter and other vessels, and for physic you shall need no other but a pound of Doctor Wrighte's Electarium lenitium, and his direction to use it, a gallon of juice of scurvy grass to drink a little [of], five or six mornings, together with some saltpeter dissolved in it, and a little grated or sliced nutmeg.

Thou must be sure to bring no more company than so many as shall have full provision for a year and a half, for though the earth here be very fertile, yet there must be time and means to raise it. If we have corn enough we may live plentifully. Yet all these are but the means which God hath ordained to do us good by. Our eyes must be towards Him, who as He can withhold blessing from the strongest means, so He can give sufficient virtue to the weakest.

I am so straightened with much business as can no way satisfy myself in writing to thee. The Lord will in due time let us see the faces of each other again to our great comfort. Now the Lord in mercy bless, guide, and support thee. I kiss and embrace thee, my dear wife. I kiss and bless you all, my dear children, Forth, Mary, Dean, Sam, and the other. The Lord keep you all and work His true fear in your hearts. The blessing of the Lord be upon all my servants, whom salute from me: Jo[hn] Sanford, Amy, etc.,

bestowed: placed in storage

boatswain: ship's officer in charge of the deck crew

quartermasters: officers in charge of quarters, clothing, equipment, etc.

physic: medicine

scurvy grass: arctic plant of the crucifer family

saltpeter: a kind of salt

straightened: stressed

augers: narrow tools for boring

Goldston, Pease, Chote, etc., my good friends at Castlins, and all my good neighbors, Goodman Cole and his good wife, and all the rest.

Remember to come well furnished with linen, woolen, some more bedding, brass, pewter, leather bottles, drinking horns, etc. Let my son provide twelve axes of several sorts of the Braintree smith or some other prime workman, whatever they cost, and some augers great and small, and many other necessaries which I can't now think of, as candle, soap, and store of beef suet, etc. Once again, farewell, my dear wife.

Thy faithful husband,
Jo: Winthrop.

Discussion Questions

1. **What thoughts do you imagine Margaret Winthrop had when she received the letter?**
2. **What would she have had to do to prepare for her family's journey?**

Some students may want to write an imaginary letter from Margaret Winthrop back to her husband.

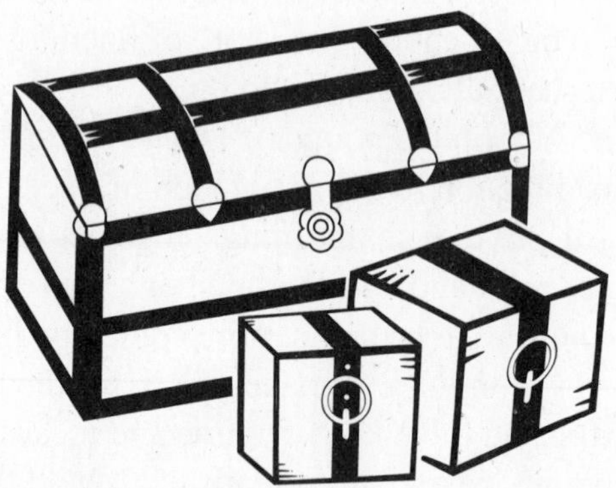

A Letter from

William Penn

On August 18, 1681, William Penn wrote to the Lenni Lenape tribe, offering to treat them and the other Iroquois tribes fairly. As a Quaker, Penn was opposed to war and was enthusiastic about peacefully coexisting with the Native Americans in Pennsylvania. Here is part of the letter.

My Friends, There is one great God and power that hath made the world and all things therein, to whom you and I, and all people owe their being and well-being, and to whom you and I must one day give an account for all that we do in the world; this great God hath written his law in our hearts, by which we are taught and commanded to love and help, and do good to one another, and not to do harm and mischief one to another. Now this great God hath been pleased to make me concerned in your parts of the world, and the king of the country where I live hath given me a great province, but I desire to enjoy it with your love and consent, that we may always live together as neighbors and friends, else what would the great God say to us, who hath made us not to devour and destroy one another, but live soberly and kindly together in the world? Now I would have you well observe, that I am very sensible of the unkindness and injustice that hath been too much exercised toward you by the people of these parts of the world, who sought themselves, and to make great advantage by you, rather than be examples of justice and goodness unto you, which I hear hath been matter of trouble to you, and caused great grudgings and animosities, sometimes to the shedding of blood, which hath made the great God angry; but I am not such a man, as is well known in my own country; I have great love and regard towards you, and I desire to win and gain your love and friendship, by a kind, just, and peaceable life, and the people I send are of the same mind, and shall in all things behave themselves accordingly.

province: an administrative division of a country

animosities: strong dislikes, ill will

Discussion Questions

1. **Do you find evidence of William Penn's Quaker beliefs in this letter? Explain.**
2. **How do you think the Lenni Lenape reacted to this letter?**

The Village Blacksmith

by Henry Wadsworth Longfellow

A blacksmith is someone who works with iron. Longfellow wrote this ballad or psalm, a song of praise, for one of his Massachusetts ancestors who was a blacksmith. In it he compares life and the forge, the furnace in which the blacksmith heats and shapes the iron.

sinewy: muscular
bellows: a two-handled bag out of which air can be forced to help build a fire
sexton: church officer

Under a spreading chestnut-tree
The village smithy stands;
The smith, a mighty man is he,
With large and sinewy hands;
And the muscles of his brawny arms
Are strong as iron bands.

His hair is crisp, and black, and long,
His face is like the tan;
His brow is wet with honest sweat,
He earns whate'er he can,
And looks the whole world in the face,
For he owes not any man.

Week in, week out, from morn till night,
You can hear his bellows blow;
You can hear him swing his heavy sledge,
With measured beat and slow,
Like a sexton ringing the village bell,
When the evening sun is low.

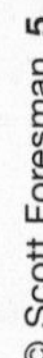

And children coming home from school
Look in at the open door;
They love to see the flaming forge,
And hear the bellows roar,
And catch the burning sparks that fly
Like chaff from a threshing-floor.

chaff: husks, or coverings, of grain that are separated from the grain during threshing

He goes on Sunday to the church,
And sits among his boys;
He hears the parson pray and preach,
He hears his daughter's voice,
Singing in the village choir,
And it makes his heart rejoice.

It sounds to him like her mother's voice,
Singing in Paradise!
He needs must think of her once more,
How in the grave she lies;
And with his hard, rough hand he wipes
A tear out of his eyes.

Toiling,—rejoicing,—sorrowing,
Onward through life he goes;
Each morning sees some task begin,
Each evening sees it close;
Something attempted, something done,
Has earned a night's repose.

Thanks, thanks to thee, my worthy friend,
For the lesson thou hast taught!
Thus at the flaming forge of life
Our fortunes must be wrought;
Thus on its sounding anvil shaped
Each burning deed and thought.

Discussion Questions

1. **Would you have liked to watch the blacksmith? Why or why not?**
2. **What do you think it means to say the blacksmith "looks the whole world in the face"?**

Students may enjoy researching the subject of blacksmithing, either online or using library books.

from

The Captive

by Joyce Hansen

Joyce Hansen wrote *The Captive,* a work of historical fiction, from the first-person point of view, as though she were a captive enslaved girl living in eighteenth-century America. In the excerpt below, she describes the life-threatening conditions aboard the slave ship and her arrival in Boston.

Ten children had survived, including myself, Joseph, and Tim. Most of the sailors must have died, for I saw only a few of them after the storm. I huddled in a corner with the other children as the remaining crew spent the rest of the day repairing the sails and cleaning the ship.

A few days after the storm, I began to notice a smell of sickness and death covering the ship like a shroud. "It's the pox," Joseph told me. I saw no more children my age. The only ones left were five girls who had seen fourteen or fifteen seasons.

Each day, more corpses were thrown overboard. Those children who had been lying near me all died. The men who worked on the ship began to cover their noses and mouths with cloths. Many of them, too, were taken ill and were dying from the sickness aboard the ship.

Lethargy seemed to have overtaken everyone. The men did not drink and sing or make Timothy and Joseph fight. The fat cook boiled his gruel in his cauldron slowly, not screaming for Joseph as he usually did. The other men moved slowly about their tasks. The wind itself was lazy, just barely ruffling the sails. The captain was not bellowing like a bull, but remained in his quarters. The man whom I called the bringer of death, because each time he examined someone the body was sent over the side of the ship, looked frightened himself.

When the skies and water turned from blue to gray and the air became frigid, I entered a bitter and bleak new world.

Boston, Massachusetts
November 1788

I pulled my blanket tightly around my shoulders and trembled so hard I thought that my teeth would fall out of my mouth. Never had I felt such cold nor seen such a gray sky. I was convinced that the evil spirits had won the battle at sea and we had been taken to their side.

When land could be seen in the distance, the crewmen pulled in the ragged sails, and the ship remained on the waters far away from shore. Joseph, Tim, and the remaining crew scrubbed the decks, hammered torn planks of wood back into place, and mended the sails while the cook cleaned his cauldron and pans.

Until nightfall, I shivered and huddled with the girls on deck under the blankets the sailors had given us. Then the crewmen unfurled the sails, and we headed for shore. I was certain that all of my clan prayed for my spirit and for my safe return to them or to my ancestors. Maybe I would find my father or Manu or even Kwesi here. I tried to be brave.

Before we stepped off the ship, a crewman gave us hard leather shoes. They looked as if they would torture my feet, as I was used to wearing soft, goatskin sandals. At first I shook my head, refusing them, but the moment my bare feet touched the icy gangplank, I put them on. The cold seeped through every inch of my body.

The captain and several sailors led all of us, including Tim and Joseph, down the narrow, cobblestone streets. One of the sailors carried a lantern, and I nervously stepped away from the frightening shadows of the square wooden buildings that lined the streets. Joseph saw the fear in my eyes and patted me on the shoulders, saying "good," which meant do not worry. The men hurried us along. They took quick glances over their shoulders, as if they were trying to hide something. I wished that Joseph could speak Ashanti so that he could tell me what was happening.

We entered a large, wooden structure, and I immediately smelled the scent of horses. I looked around and saw a row of stalls with horses behind them. Did people in this place keep animals inside their homes? I studied the wooden walls and dirt floor covered with hay and wondered what kind of home this was. Where were the brightly colored rugs to sit on and baskets to put clothing in? How could people sleep in the same smelly room with animals?

clan: group or tribe
Ashanti: an African language

Discussion Questions

1. **How does this fictional passage help you understand the experience of being a captured African?**
2. **What do you think the enslaved girl misses most about her home?**

from

Calico Bush

by Rachel Field

In *Calico Bush*, a historical novel, Rachel Field describes the emotions and thoughts of Marguerite Ledoux, a twelve-year-old "bound out" French girl. A "bound out" person was required to work off his or her debt (often the cost of passage from Europe to America) in service to a person or family. Since Marguerite has no guardian after her grandmother dies, she is bound out to a family that needs a servant. In the excerpt below, Marguerite and the Sargent family are on a boat. The "treasures" on the cord that Marguerite tucks out of sight are a gold ring of her grandmother's and a gilt button from her uncle's best coat.

People had been kind to her when Grand'mere died, but afterwards they had explained that life would be very different. It was not enough, it appeared, for one to know songs and dancing steps and how to sew and embroider. This was a new, rough country with very different sort of work to be done, and an able-bodied girl of twelve must earn her "board and keep." She remembered what a frightening sound those same words had had. And then they had explained to her that she was to be a "Bound-out Girl." Already those in authority were searching about for a family who would take her to work for them. But the fact that she was French had stood in her way. Several women had come to look her over, only to dismiss her with headshakes when they discovered her birth.

"We want no flighty foreign critters under our roof," she had heard one woman say.

The other had expressed like disapproval and had even hinted that with King George at war with the French across the water, she wouldn't feel she was doing her duty to consort with the enemy. But Joel Sargent and Dolly had not been so particular.

"Another pair of hands and feet are what we're in need of," they had explained, "and so long's she ain't the contrary kind we'll overlook where she was born and raised."

Marguerite had sat by while the papers were being drawn up and signed. She had not understood many of the strange words and phrases, but she had not missed their meaning. From that day till her eighteenth birthday she was theirs to command. She would be answerable to these people for her every act and word, bound to serve them for six long years in return for shelter, food, and such garments as should be deemed necessary.

Hastily she slipped the cord and its treasures out of sight again and, tucking her bare feet under her, went at the wool more vigorously.

This had been in March. Now it was June. Marblehead was well behind them. Save to herself she was no longer Marguerite Ledoux but the Sargents' Bound-out Girl in gray holland and cotton sunbonnet, who answered to the name of Maggie when called.

Her mistress was calling to her now. "Here, Maggie, mind the young ones while I fetch the men some victuals. Their stomachs must be clean empty, their tongues are that quarrelsome."

Marguerite rose quickly to take the baby, and the children flocked about her in turn, their sturdy fairness in marked contrast to her own dark coloring and wiry build. Becky and Susan, the six-year-old twins, were alike as two peas in a pod, a stocky pair with stiff little braids of yellow hair and blue eyes. They too wore sunbonnets and dresses of gray holland, short in the sleeve and neck but gathered round the waist into full skirts that flapped about their bare ankles. Patty came next in order, being four, with Jacob, three, ever close at her heels. Their hair, white and curly as lambs' wool, was sheared close to their round heads, and save for Jacob's short breeches and dimpled chin they too might have passed for twins. The baby, Deborah, called Debby by them all, was eight months old and already showed tufts of light hair under her tight little cap. Her eyes were also very blue and her cheeks apple-round and rosy.

"Keep her out the sun, much as you can," the baby's mother cautioned from the cabin. "It's hot enough to raise blisters on her, and this is no place for her to run a fever, dear knows."

"Yes'm," Marguerite answered as she had been taught, crooking her arm to shade the baby's face.

"This old floor's so hot it burns my feet, it does," complained Becky, standing first on one foot and then on the other.

"You should spread your dress out," Marguerite told her; "and then if you fold your feet under you when you sit, you will not feel it."

She showed them how to do so, and they crouched beside her, all but Jacob, who climbed to the larger keg and sat with his feet stuck straight before him staring out to sea.

holland: linen or cotton used to make clothes

"Prenez garde!" Marguerite cried as the boat swung about and the child all but slid off. Then, seeing the blank looks on the small faces before her, she caught herself up quickly: "Take care to hold fast!"

"Yes," echoed Susan, "and take care the boom do not sweep you over the side when they shift it."

They were used to boats, as were most seaport children of that day, and although Jacob was only three he was expected to look out for himself. He did not, however, remain long on his perch, for Caleb, happening by, picked him off by the back of his shirt and set him down with his sisters.

"I'll send you to join the fishes if you don't watch out," he chided before he hurried over to the men about the tiller.

They were discussing charts and courses as they ate thick pieces of bread and cheese out of Dolly Sargent's basket. . . .

"There ain't no two ways about it." The Captain spoke up at last. "We'll stick to the inner course if it takes us a week from here to the Penobscot. When I said we'd go outside the shoals I didn't lot on havin' her so down by the head."

"Then we'd best put in at Falmouth, " Joel said, pointing with his big leathery forefinger to a place on the chart spread between them. "We'll be 'most out of water and feed for the critters by then."

"Yes," agreed Ira, "it'll give us all a chance to stretch our legs a bit, and Dolly won't look so glum if she knows she'll have another sight of folks and fashions."

Discussion Questions

1. **How do you think Marguerite feels about her situation?**
2. **How do you think you would feel if you were a bound-out girl or boy? Why?**

Encourage students to read all of *Calico Bush*.

from

Washington's School Exercises: Rules of Civility & Decent Behaviour

George Washington copied down these and other rules when he was about fourteen years old.

wry: twist
bedew: make wet

- Every Action done in Company, ought to be with Some Sign of Respect, to those that are Present. . . .
- Shew Nothing to your Freind that may affright him.
- In the Presence of Others Sing not to yourself with a humming Noise, nor Drum with your Fingers or Feet.
- If You Cough, Sneeze, Sigh, or Yawn, do it not Loud but Privately; and Speak not in your Yawning, but put Your handkercheif or Hand before your face and turn aside.
- Sleep not when others Speak, Sit not when others stand, Speak not when you Should hold your Peace, walk not on when others Stop. . . .
- At Play and at Fire its Good manners to Give Place to the last Commer, and affect not to Speak Louder than Ordinary.
- Spit not in the Fire, nor Stoop low before it neither Put your Hands into the Flames to warm them, nor Set your Feet upon the Fire especially if there be meat before it.
- When you Sit down, Keep your Feet firm and Even, without putting one on the other or Crossing them. . . .
- Shake not the head, Feet, or Legs rowl not the Eys lift not one eyebrow higher than the other wry not the mouth, and bedew no mans face with your Spittle, by appr[oaching too near] him [when] you Speak. . . .
- Turn not your Back to others especially in Speaking, Jog not the Table or Desk on which Another reads or writes, lean not upon any one.
- Keep your Nails clean and Short, also your Hands and Teeth Clean yet without Shewing any great Concern for them.
- Do not Puff up the Cheeks, Loll not out the tongue rub the Hands, or beard, thrust out the lips, or bite them or keep the Lips too open or too Close.
- Be no Flatterer, neither Play with any that delights not to be Play'd Withal.

nigh: near
countenance: face
superfluous: extra and unnecessary
affectation: behavior that is not natural for you

- Read no Letters, Books, or Papers in Company but when there is a Necessity for the doing of it you must ask leave: come not near the Books or Writings of Another so as to read them unless desired or give your opinion of them unask'd also look not nigh when another is writing a Letter.
- Let your Countenance be pleasant but in Serious Matters Somewhat grave.
- The gestures of the Body must be Suited to the discourse you are upon.
- Reproach none for the Infirmaties of Nature, nor Delight to Put them that have in mind thereof.
- Shew not yourself glad at the Misfortune of another though he were your enemy.
- When you see a Crime punished, you may be inwardly Pleased; but always shew Pity to the Suffering Offender. . . .
- Superfluous Complements and all Affectation of Ceremonie are to be avoided, yet where due they are not to be Neglected.
- In Pulling off your Hat to Persons of Distinction, as Noblemen, Justices, Churchmen &c make a Reverence, bowing more or less according to the Custom of the Better Bred, and Quality of the Person. . . .
- If any one come to Speak to you while you are Sitting Stand up tho he be your Inferiour, and when you Present Seats let it be to every one according to his Degree.
- When you meet with one of Greater Quality than yourself, Stop, and retire especially if it be at a Door or any Straight place to give way for him to Pass.
- In walking the highest Place in most Countrys Seems to be on the right hand therefore Place yourself on the left of him whom you desire to Honour: but if three walk together the mid [dest] Place is the most Honourable the wall is usually given to the most worthy if two walk together.

Discussion Questions

1. **Do you think it would be hard to follow all these rules? Why or why not?**
2. **What are some rules of behavior that people follow in the present day? Which ones are the same as the rules Washington wrote down? Which ones belong only in modern times?**

from

Equiano's Travels

by Olaudah Equiano

Montserrat is a French colonial island in the Caribbean. It was a port on the so-called Middle Passage, the voyage between Africa and the Americas on the triangular trade route between Europe, Africa, and America. In this excerpt from his autobiography, Olaudah Equiano describes the inhumane treatment of enslaved Africans and the dehumanizing effect of being a slave trader or slave holder.

In all the different islands in which I have been (and I have visited no less than fifteen) the treatment of the slaves was nearly the same; so nearly indeed, that the history of an island or even a plantation, with a few such exceptions as I have mentioned, might serve for a history of the whole. Such a tendency has the slave-trade to debauch men's minds and harden them to every feeling of humanity! For I will not suppose that the dealers in slaves are born worse than other men—No, it is the fatality of this mistaken avarice that it corrupts the milk of human kindness and turns it into gall. And had the pursuits of those men been different, they might have been as generous, as tender-hearted and just, as they are unfeeling, rapacious and cruel. Surely this traffic cannot be good, which spreads like a pestilence and taints what it touches! which violates that first natural right of mankind, equality and independency, and gives one man a dominion over his fellows which God could never intend! For it raises the owner to a state as far above man as it depresses the slave below it, and with all the presumption of human pride, sets a distinction between them, immeasurable in extent and endless in duration! Yet how mistaken is the avarice even of the planters! Are slaves more useful by being thus humbled to the condition of brutes than they would be if suffered to enjoy the privileges of men? The freedom which diffuses health and prosperity throughout Britain answers you—No. When you make men slaves you deprive them of half their virtue, you set them in your own conduct an example of fraud, rapine, and cruelty, and compel them to live with you in a state of war, and yet you complain that they are not honest or faithful! You stupefy them with stripes and think it necessary to keep them in a state of ignorance, and yet you assert that they are incapable of learning, that their minds are such a barren soil or moor that culture would be lost on

debauch: lead astray

avarice: greed

gall: bitterness

taints: poisons

rapine: seizing and carrying off things by force

stripes: whippings that raise long welts on the skin

prodigal: generous

them, and that they come from a climate where nature, though prodigal of her bounties in a degree unknown to yourselves, has left man alone scant and unfinished and incapable of enjoying the treasures she had poured out for him!—An assertion at once impious and absurd. Why do you use those instruments of torture? Are they fit to be applied by one rational being to another? And are ye not struck with shame and mortification to see the partakers of your nature reduced so low? But above all, are there no dangers attending this mode of treatment? Are you not hourly in dread of an insurrection? Nor would it be surprising: for when

"—No peace is given
To us enslav'd, but custody severe;
And stripes and arbitrary punishment
Inflicted—What peace can we return?
But to our power, hostility and hate;
Untam'd reluctance, and revenge, though slow.
Yet ever plotting how the conqueror least
May reap his conquest, and may least rejoice
In doing what we most in suffering feel."

But by changing your conduct and treating your slaves as men every cause of fear would be banished. They would be faithful, honest, intelligent and vigorous; and peace, prosperity, and happiness, would attend you.

Discussion Questions

1. **Did Equiano wish to inform or persuade others? Explain.**
2. **Do you agree with Equiano that, above all, a slaveholder should be afraid of rebellion? Explain your opinion.**

from

Great River: The Rio Grande

by Paul Horgan

During the Pueblo Revolt against the Spanish in New Mexico, the Spanish governor was given a warning by a Pueblo Indian named John (or Juan). This excerpt describes the events that took place around the town of Santa Fe some days before and on the day of that warning.

It was clear then that the revolt had been planned as a coordinated effort, and the Governor was certain that the Indians meant to destroy every Spaniard in the kingdom. He summoned all who could to come to the Palace. By Monday night, the twelfth of August, many people had come to take refuge from Indians. . . .

At nine the next morning, across the Santa Fe creek in the fields around the chapel of Saint Michael moved what the watchers barricaded in the Palace dreaded to see. Rattling through the cornfields came a painted host, some on horseback, some on foot, making cries for blood. They were armed with native weapons and with Spanish harquebuses, lances, swords and padded jackets which they had taken from the dead. There were dwellings in the fields and these the invading Indians entered and sacked, making barracks of them where they would await reinforcements from other pueblos. One of them was an Indian called John whom the Spaniards knew. The Governor sent an escort of soldiers to bring him to the Palace under safe-conduct. Riding his horse, and wearing about his waist a red taffeta ribbon which had been torn from the missal of Galisteo, he was outfitted with a full complement of Spanish arms. Carrying two crosses, one white, one red, he came to speak to the Governor in the patio of the Palace.

host: army
harquebuses: heavy guns
missal: book of prayers and readings used during a Roman Catholic Mass
complement: complete set

friars: Catholic clergy

"John," said the Governor, "why have you too gone crazy when you are an Indian who speaks our tongue, who are so intelligent, who have lived all your life in the capital with us, where I placed so much confidence in you? And now look at you: a leader of the Indian rebels!"

"They elected me their captain," replied John. "They sent these two crosses to show you. This one"—the white—"means peace. And the other one, war."

"Well?"

"If you choose the white there will be no war but you must all leave the country. If you choose the red, you must all die, for we are many and you are few. Having killed so many Spaniards and priests, we will kill all the rest."

The Governor spoke to him "very persuasively," saying:

"Now John, you and the rest of your followers are all Catholic Christians. How do you expect to live without your friars? Even if you have committed so many crimes already, there can still be pardon, if you will return to obedience. Now go back and tell your friends, in my name, what I have said, and tell them they should accept it, and go to their homes quietly. And then come back and tell me what they say."

John left and returned. His answer was dishonest, asking that all classes of Indians in the Spanish service be given up, that his wife and children be allowed to join him, and that all Apache men and women who were prisoners of the Spanish be released, as Apaches among the rebels were asking for them. Lacking these things, war would follow immediately. But there were no Apaches among them, and the Governor knew it. John was only playing for time until allies arrived to join him from Taos, Picuries and the Tewa pueblos. The Governor dismissed him to go back and say that unless the outrages in the fields of San Miguel ceased at once, the soldiers would be ordered forth to attack. John went back across the creek with this word, and when he spoke it, the Indians joined in a howl of rage, and rang the bells of Saint Michael's and blew trumpets, in defiance, and moved toward the Palace.

Discussion Questions

1. **How do you think the Governor felt when he saw the Pueblo Indian wearing a red ribbon torn from a prayer book?**
2. **What do you think of the choice that the Pueblo offered the Governor?**

To learn more about the history of the Pueblo Indians, students can go online, read books in the library, or interview experts about Southwestern Indian tribes.

A Letter from

Junípero Serra to Father Palu

Twenty-one years after Junípero Serra emigrated from Spain to Mexico as a Catholic missionary, he traveled to the port of San Diego, California, with a group of Indian and Spanish families. He wrote the letter below, dated July 3, 1769, to Father Palu, his future biographer.

My Dear Friend:—Thank God I arrived the day before yesterday, the first of the month, at this port of San Diego, truly a fine one, and not without reason called famous. Here I found those who had set out before me, both by sea and land, except those who have died. The brethren, Fathers Cresp, Vizcaino, Parron and Gomez, are here with myself, and all are quite well, thank God. Here are also the two vessels, but the San Carlos without sailors, all having died of the scurvy, except two. The San Antonio, although she sailed a month and a half later, arrived twenty days before the San Carlos, losing on the voyage eight sailors. In consequence of this loss, it has been resolved that the San Antonio shall return to San Blas, to fetch sailors for herself and for the San Carlos.

brethren: brothers
vessels: boats
scurvy: disease caused by lack of vitamin C
procure: get

The causes of the delay of the San Carlos were: first, lack of water, owing to the casks being bad, which, together, with bad water obtained on the coast, occasioned sickness among the crew; and secondly, the error which all were in respecting the situation of this port. They supposed it to be thirty-three or thirty-four degrees north latitude, some saying one and some the other, and strict orders were given to Captain Villa and the rest to keep out in the open sea till they arrived at the thirty-fourth degree, and then to make the shore in search of the port. As, however, the port in reality lies in thirty-two degrees thirty-four minutes, according to the observations that have been made, they went much beyond it, thus making the voyage much longer than was necessary. The people got daily worse from the cold and the bad water, and they must all have perished if they had not discovered the port about the time they did. For they were quite unable to launch the boat to procure more water, or to do anything whatever for their preservation. Father Fernando did everything in his power to assist the sick; and although he arrived much reduced in flesh, he did not become ill, and is now well. We

rivulets: small rivers

Castile: large region of north and central Spain, center of the Spanish monarchy in Serra's time

victuals: food

have not suffered hunger or other privations, neither have the Indians who came with us; all arrived well and healthy.

The tract through which we passed is generally very good land, with plenty of water; and there, as well as here, the country is neither rocky nor overrun with brushwood. There are, however, many hills, but they are composed of earth. The road has been good in some places, but the greater part bad. About half-way, the valleys and banks of rivulets began to be delightful. We found vines of a large size, and in some cases quite loaded with grapes; we also found an abundance of roses, which appeared to be like those of Castile.

We have seen Indians in immense numbers, and all those on this coast of the Pacific contrive to make a good subsistence on various seeds, and by fishing. The latter they carry on by means of rafts or canoes, made of tule (bullrush) with which they go a great way to sea. They are very civil. . . . We found on our journey, as well as in the place where we stopped, that they treated us with as much confidence and good-will as if they had known us all their lives. But when we offered them any of our victuals, they always refused them. All they cared for was cloth, and only for something of this sort would they exchange their fish or whatever else they had. During the whole march we found hares, rabbits, some deer, and a multitude of berendos (a kind of a wild goat).

I pray God may preserve your health and life many years.

From this port and intended Mission of San Diego, in North California, third July, 1769.

Fr. Junípero Serra.

Discussion Questions

1. **If you had traveled with Father Serra, what would have appealed to you about the land you were marching through?**
2. **Why do you think these Pacific Coast Indians were friendly to Serra?**

from

Voyages of Marquette

by Jacques Marquette

This journal entry by French missionary Jacques Marquette describes his encounter with the Illinois tribe on his first voyage down the Mississippi in 1673.

clad: clothed
devoured: took in greedily
profound: deep

Finally, when they had drawn near, they stopped to Consider us attentively. I was reassured when I observed these Ceremonies, which with them are performed only among friends; and much more so when I saw them Clad in Cloth, for I judged thereby that they were our allies. I therefore spoke to them first, and asked them who they were. They replied that they were Ilinois and, as a token of peace, they offered us their pipes to smoke. They afterward invited us to enter their Village, where all the people impatiently awaited us. These pipes for smoking tobacco are called in This country Calumets. This word has come so much Into use that, in order to be understood, I shall be obliged to use it, as I shall often have to mention these pipes.

Section 5th. How the Ilinois Received the Father in Their Village.

At the Door of the Cabin in which we were to be received was an old man, who awaited us in a rather surprising attitude, which constitutes a part of the Ceremonial that they observe when they receive Strangers. This man stood . . . with his hands extended and lifted toward the sun, As if he wished to protect himself from its rays, which nevertheless shone upon his face through his fingers. When we came near him, he paid us This Compliment: "How beautiful the sun is, O frenchman, when thou comest to visit us! All our village awaits thee, and thou shalt enter all our Cabins in peace." Having said this, he made us enter his own, in which were a crowd of people; they devoured us with their eyes, but, nevertheless, observed profound silence. We could however, hear these words, which were addressed to us from time to time in a low voice: "How good it is, My brothers, that you should visit us."

Discussion Questions

1. **How would you describe Marquette's reception by the Illinois?**
2. **What gestures of welcome or greeting are used when strangers or groups of strangers visit each other today?**

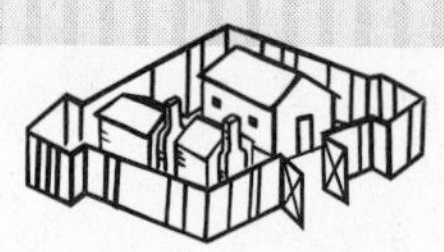

A Letter from

George Washington to His Mother

In this July 18, 1755, letter excerpt, George Washington describes his defeat near Fort Duquesne while he was fighting for the British against the French and their Indian allies.

Inst.: abbreviation for instant, in the present month
stragler: straggler
Scoutg. Ind'ns: scouting Indians
dastardly: mean and cowardly

Honour'd Mad'm: As I doubt not but you have heard of our defeat, and perhaps have it represented in a worse light (if possible) than it deserves; I have taken this earliest opportunity to give you some acct. of the Engagement, as it happen'd within 7 miles of the French Fort, on Wednesday the 9th Inst.

We March'd on to that place with't any considerable loss, having only now and then a stragler pick'd up by the French Scoutg. Ind'ns. When we came there, we were attack'd by a Body of French and Indns. whose number, (I am certain) did not exceed 300 Men; our's consisted of abt. 1,300 well arm'd Troops; chiefly of the English Soldiers, who were struck with such a panick, that they behav'd with more cowardice than it is possible to conceive; The Officers behav'd Gallantly in order to encourage their Men, for which they suffer'd greatly; there being near 60 kill'd and wounded; a large proportion out of the number we had! The Virginia Troops shew'd a good deal of Bravery, and were near all kill'd; for I believe out of 3 Companys that were there, there is scarce 30 Men left alive; Capt. Peyrouny and all his Officer's down to a Corporal was kill'd; Capt. Polson shar'd near as hard a Fate; for only one of his was left: In short the dastardly behaviour of those they call regular's expos'd all others that were inclin'd to do their duty to almost certain death; and at last, in dispight of all the efforts of the Officer's to the Contrary, they broke and run as Sheep pursued by dogs; and it was impossible to rally them.

The Genl. was wounded; of w'ch he died 3 Days after; Sir Peter Halket was kill'd in the Field where died many other brave Officer's; I luckily escap'd with't a wound, tho' I had four Bullets through my Coat, and two Horses shot under me.

Discussion Questions

1. **How do you suppose Washington's mother reacted to the news in this letter?**
2. **Do you think people nowadays still want to write and receive personal letters? Why or why not?**

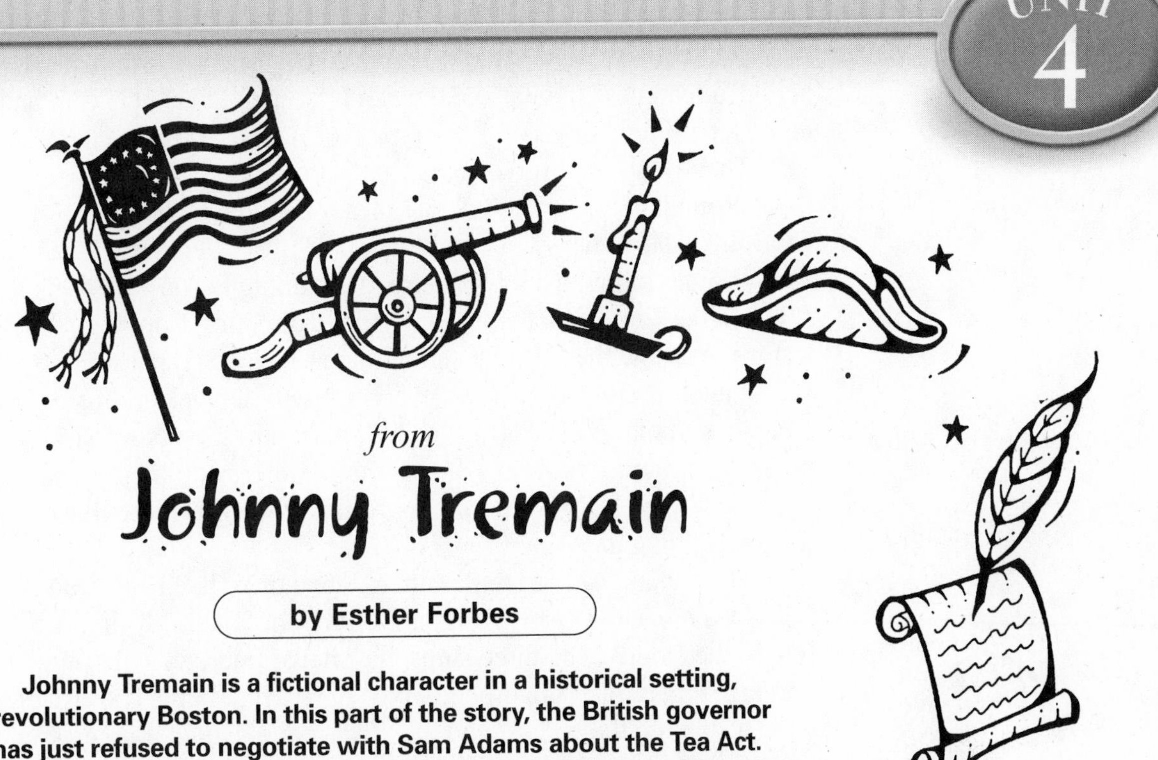

from

Johnny Tremain

by Esther Forbes

Johnny Tremain is a fictional character in a historical setting, revolutionary Boston. In this part of the story, the British governor has just refused to negotiate with Sam Adams about the Tea Act. Johnny and his friends are ready to carry out the Patriot plan to dress as Mohawk Indians and dump the British tea into Boston Harbor.

And suddenly there was silence. Johnny guessed there were many in that crowd who, like himself, were hanging on those words. Seemingly Mr. Adams was calmly accepting defeat, dismissing the meeting, for now he was saying,

'This meeting can do nothing more to save the country.'

Johnny gave his first shrill blast on his whistle, and he heard whistles and cries seemingly in all directions, Indian war whoops and 'Boston Harbor a teapot tonight!' 'Hurrah for Griffin's Wharf!' 'Salt-water tea!' 'Hi, Mohawks, get your axes and pay no taxes!'

Johnny was only afraid all would be over before Rab and his henchmen could get to the wharf. Still shrilling on the whistle, he fought and floundered against the tide of the crowd. It was sweeping toward Griffin's Wharf, he struggling to get back to Salt Lane. Now he was afraid the others would have gone on without him. After all, Rab might have decided that Johnny's legs and ears were better than his hands—and deliberately let him do the work that best suited him. Johnny pushed open the door.

Rab was alone. He had Johnny's blanket coat, his ridiculous befeathered knitted cap in his hands.

'Quick!' he said, and smootched his face with soot, drew a red line across his mouth running from ear to ear. Johnny saw Rab's eyes through the mask of soot. They were glowing with that dark excitement he had seen but twice before. His lips were parted. His teeth looked sharp and white as an animal's. In spite of his calm demeanor, calm voice, he was charged and surcharged with a will to action, a readiness to take and enjoy any desperate chance. Rab had come terrifyingly alive.

They flung themselves out of the shop.

'Roundabout!' cried Rab. He meant they would get to the wharf by back alleys.

'Come, follow me. *Now* we're really going to run.'

He flew up Salt Lane in the opposite direction from the waterfront. Now they were flinging themselves down back alleys (faster and faster). Once they had a glimpse of a blacksmith shop and other 'Indians' clamoring for soot for their faces. Now slipping over a back-yard fence, now at last on the waterfront, Sea Street, Flounder Alley. They were running so fast it seemed more like a dream of flying than reality.

The day had started with rain and then there had been clouds, but as they reached Griffin's Wharf the moon, full and white, broke free of the clouds. The three ships, the silent hundreds gathering upon the wharf, all were dipped in the pure white light. The crowds were becoming thousands, and there was not one there but guessed what was to be done, and all approved.

Rab was grunting out of the side of his mouth to a thick set, active-looking man, whom Johnny would have known anywhere, by his walk and the confident lift of his head, was Mr. Revere. 'Me Know You.'

'Me Know You,' Johnny repeated this countersign and took his place behind Mr. Revere. The other boys, held up by the crowd, began arriving, and more men and boys. But Johnny guessed that many who were now quietly joining one of those three groups were acting on the spur of the moment, seeing what was up. They had blacked their faces, seized axes, and come along. They were behaving as quietly and were as obedient to their leaders as those who had been so carefully picked for this work of destruction.

There was a boatswain's whistle, and in silence one group boarded the *Dartmouth*. The *Eleanor* and the *Beaver* had to be warped in to the wharf. Johnny was close to Mr. Revere's heels. He heard him calling for the captain, promising him, in the jargon everyone talked that night, that not one thing should be damaged on the ship except only the tea, but the captain and all his crew had best stay in the cabin until the work was over.

Captain Hall shrugged and did as he was told, leaving his cabin boy to hand over the keys to the hold. The boy was grinning with pleasure. The 'tea party' was not unexpected.

'I'll show you,' the boy volunteered, 'how to work them hoists. I'll fetch lanterns, mister.'

The winches rattled and the heavy chests began to appear—one hundred and fifty of them. As some men worked in the hold, others broke open the chests and flung the tea into the harbor. But one thing made them unexpected difficulty. The tea inside the chests was wrapped in heavy canvas. The axes went through the wood easily enough—the canvas made endless trouble. Johnny had never worked so hard in his life.

He had noticed a stout boy with a blackened face working near him. The boy looked familiar, but when he saw his white, fat hands, Johnny knew who he was and kept a sharp eye on him. It was Dove. He was not one of the original 'Indians,' but a volunteer. He had on an enormous pair of breeches tied at each knee with rope. Even as Johnny opened a chest and helped get the tea over the rail, he kept an eye on Dove. The boy was secretly scooping tea into his breeches. This theft would come to several hundred dollars in value, but more important it would ruin the high moral tone of the party. Johnny whispered to Rab, who put down the axe he had been wielding with such passion and grabbed Dove. It wasn't much of a scuffle. Soon Dove was whining and admitting that a little of the tea had happened to 'splash' into his breeches. Johnny got them off and kicked them and the many pounds of tea they held into the harbor.

'He swim good,' he grunted at Rab, for everyone was talking 'Indian' that night.

Rab picked up the fat Dove as though he were a rag baby and flung him into the harbor. The tea was thicker than any seaweed and its fragrance was everywhere.

Not a quarter of a mile away, quite visible in the moonlight, rode the *Active* and the *Kingfisher*. Any moment the tea party might be interrupted by British marines. There was no landing party. Governor Hutchinson had been wise in not sending for their help.

The work on the *Dartmouth* and the *Eleanor* finished about the same time. The *Beaver* took longer, for she had not had time to unload the rest of her cargo, and great care was taken not to injure it. Just as Johnny was about to go over to see if he could help on the *Beaver*, Mr. Revere whispered to him. 'Go get brooms. Clean um' deck.'

Johnny and a parcel of boys brushed the deck until it was clean as a parlor floor. Then Mr. Revere called the captain to come up and inspect. The tea was utterly gone, but Captain Hall agreed that beyond that there had not been the slightest damage.

Discussion Questions

1. **How do you think Johnny and Rab felt during this event?**
2. **This book was first published in 1943. How do you think the author got the information needed to write the book?**

from

"Give Me Liberty or Give Me Death" Speech

by Patrick Henry

In this speech, Henry tells the Virginia Provincial Convention that British armies and navies are increasing in the colonies and that begging the King for liberty has not worked.

There is no longer any room for hope. If we wish to be free—if we mean to preserve inviolate those inestimable privileges for which we have been so long contending—if we mean not basely to abandon the noble struggle in which we have been so long engaged, and which we have pledged ourselves never to abandon until the glorious object of our contest be obtained—we must fight! I repeat it, sir, we must fight! An appeal to arms, and to the God of hosts, is all that is left us! . . .

We shall not fight our battles alone. There is a just God who presides over the destinies of nations; and who will raise up friends to fight our battles for us. The battle, sir, is not to the strong alone; it is to the vigilant, the active, the brave. Besides, sir, we have no election. If we were base enough to desire it, it is now too late to retire from the contest. There is no retreat but in submission and slavery! Our chains are forged. Their clanking may be heard on the plains of Boston! The war is inevitable and let it come! I repeat, sir, let it come!!

It is in vain, sir, to extenuate the matter. Gentlemen may cry peace, peace—but there is no peace. The war is actually begun! The next gale that sweeps from the north will bring to our ears the clash of resounding arms! Our brethren are already in the field! Why stand we here idle? What is it that gentlemen wish? What would they have? Is life so dear, or peace so sweet, as to be purchased at the price of chains and slavery? Forbid it, Almighty God!—I Know not what course others may take, but as for me, give me liberty or give me death!

Discussion Questions

1. **Did Patrick Henry wish to inform or persuade others? How do you know?**
2. **How did Patrick Henry feel about the situation between England and the colonies?**

Paul Revere's Ride

by Henry Wadsworth Longfellow

Longfellow wrote this poem almost ninety years after Paul Revere's famous ride. The poem, like the novel *Johnny Tremain,* is partly fiction. Yet it puts the listener into the moment, recreating the drama of the ride with figurative language ("windows that can see") and sensory images ("bleating of the flock").

Listen, my children, and you shall hear
Of the midnight ride of Paul Revere,
On the eighteenth of April, in Seventy-five;
Hardly a man is now alive
Who remembers that famous day and year.

He said to his friend, "If the British march
By land or sea from the town tonight,
Hang a lantern aloft in the belfry arch
Of the North Church tower as a signal light,—
One, if by land, and two, if by sea;
And I on the opposite shore will be,
Ready to ride and spread the alarm
Through every Middlesex village and farm,
For the country folk to be up and to arm."

Then he said, "Good night!" and with muffled oar
Silently rowed to the Charlestown shore,
Just as the moon rose over the bay,
Where swinging wide at her moorings lay
The *Somerset*, British man-of-war;
A phantom ship, with each mast and spar
Across the moon like a prison bar,
And a huge black hulk, that was magnified
By its own reflection in the tide.

Meanwhile, his friend, through alley and street,
Wanders and watches with eager ears,
Till in the silence around him he hears
The muster of men at the barrack door,
The sound of arms, and the tramp of feet,
And the measured tread of the grenadiers,
Marching down to their boats on the shore.

Then he climbed the tower of the Old North Church,
By the wooden stairs, with stealthy tread,
To the belfry-chamber overhead,
And startled the pigeons from their perch
On the somber rafters, that 'round him made
Masses and moving shapes of shade,—
By the trembling ladder, steep and tall,
To the highest window in the wall,
Where he paused to listen and look down
A moment on the roofs of the town,
And the moonlight flowing over all.

Beneath, in the churchyard, lay the dead,
In their night-encampment on the hill,
Wrapped in silence so deep and still
That he could hear, like a sentinel's tread,
The watchful night-wind, as it went
Creeping along from tent to tent,
And seeming to whisper, "All is well!"
A moment only he feels the spell
Of the place and the hour, and the secret dread
Of the lonely belfry and the dead;
For suddenly all his thoughts are bent
On a shadowy something far away,
Where the river widens to meet the bay,—
A line of black that bends and floats
On the rising tide, like a bridge of boats.

Meanwhile, impatient to mount and ride,
Booted and spurred, with a heavy stride
On the opposite shore walked Paul Revere.
Now he patted his horse's side,
Now gazed at the landscape far and near,
Then, impetuous, stamped the earth,
And turned and tightened his saddle-girth;
But mostly he watched with eager search
The belfry-tower of the Old North Church,
As it rose above the graves on the hill,

Lonely and spectral and somber and still.
And lo! As he looks, on the belfry's height
A glimmer, and then a gleam of light!
He springs to the saddle, the bridle he turns,
But lingers and gazes, till full on his sight
A second lamp in the belfry burns!

A hurry of hoofs in a village street,
A shape in the moonlight, a bulk in the dark,
And beneath, from the pebbles, in passing, a spark
Struck out by a steed flying fearless and fleet;
That was all! And yet, through the gloom and the light,
The fate of a nation was riding that night;
And the spark struck out by that steed in his flight,
Kindled the land into flame with its heat.

He has left the village and mounted the steep,
And beneath him, tranquil and broad and deep,
Is the Mystic, meeting the ocean tides;
And under the alders, that skirt its edge,
Now soft on the sand, now loud on the ledge,
Is heard the tramp of his steed as he rides.

Mystic: a river that flows into Boston Harbor

It was twelve by the village clock
When he crossed the bridge into Medford town,
He heard the crowing of the cock,
And the barking of the farmer's dog,
And felt the damp of the river fog,
That rises after the sun goes down.

It was one by the village clock,
When he galloped into Lexington.
He saw the gilded weathercock
Swim in the moonlight as he passed,
And the meeting-house windows, blank and bare,
Gaze at him with a spectral glare,
As if they already stood aghast
At the bloody work they would look upon.

It was two by the village clock,
When he came to the bridge in Concord town.
He heard the bleating of the flock,
And the twitter of birds among the trees,
And felt the breath of the morning breeze
Blowing over the meadows brown.
And one was safe and asleep in his bed
Who at the bridge would be first to fall,
Who at the bridge would be lying dead,
Pierced by a British musket-ball.

You know the rest. In the books you have read,
How the British Regulars fired and fled,—
How the farmers gave them ball for ball,
From behind each fence and farmyard wall,
Chasing the redcoats down the lane,
Then crossing the fields to emerge again
Under the trees at the turn of the road,
And only pausing to fire and load.

So through the night rode Paul Revere;
And so through the night went his cry of alarm
To every Middlesex village and farm, —
A cry of defiance, and not of fear,
A voice in the darkness, a knock at the door,
And a word that shall echo forevermore!
For, borne on the night-wind of the Past,
Through all our history, to the last,
In the hour of darkness and peril and need,
The people will waken and listen to hear
The hurrying hoofbeats of that steed,
And the midnight message of Paul Revere.

Discussion Questions

1. **Was the poet a neutral recorder of history, or did personal opinions or interests influence what he wrote? How do you know?**
2. **What does the poet mean by "And the spark struck out by that steed in his flight,/Kindled the land into flame with its heat"?**

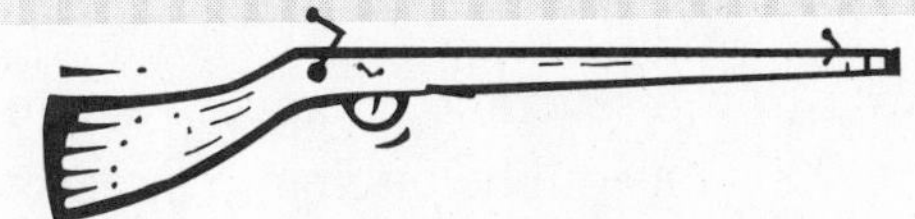

The Battles of Lexington and Concord

These two newspaper articles both report on the battles of Lexington and Concord. One is dated April 25, 1775, six days after the battles, and was published in Salem, Massachusetts, a large colonial town near the battle sites. The other is dated June 10, 1775, more than a month after the battles, and was published in London, England, an ocean away from the battle sites.

from
The Essex Gazette

admit: allow
expedition: speed
rod: a distance of 5.5 yards

SALEM, April 25.

Last Wednesday, the 19th of April, the Troops of his Britannick Majesty commenced Hostilities upon the People of this Province, attended with Circumstances of Cruelty not less brutal than what our venerable Ancestors received from the vilest Savages of the Wilderness. The Particulars relative to this interesting Event, by which we are involved in all the Horrors of a civil War, we have endeavored to collect as well as the present confused State of Affairs will admit.

On Tuesday Evening a Detachment from the Army, consisting, it is said, of 8 or 900 Men, commanded by Lieut. Col. Smith, embarked at the Bottom of the Common in Boston, on board a Number of Boats, and landed at Phips's Farm, a little Way up Charles River, from whence they proceeded with Silence and Expedition, on their Way to Concord, about 18 Miles from Boston. The People were soon alarmed, and began to assemble, in several Towns before Day-Light, in order to watch the Motion of the Troops. At Lexington, 6 Miles below Concord, a Company of Militia, of about 100 Men, mustered near the Meeting House; the Troops came in Sight of them just before Sun-rise; and running within a few Rods of them, the Commanding Officer accosted the Militia in Words to this Effect:—

"Disperse you Rebels— . . . , throw down your Arms and disperse:" Upon which the Troops huzza'd, and immediately one or two Officers discharged their Pistols, which were instantaneously followed by the firing of 4 or 5 of the Soldiers, and then there seemed to be a general Discharge from the whole Body: Eight of our Men were killed, and nine wounded. In a few Minutes after this Action the Enemy renewed their March for Concord, at which Place

Chaises: two-wheeled carriages
Precipitation: haste
Field Pieces: cannons
Consternation: confused dismay

they destroyed several Carriages, Carriage Wheels, and about 20 Barrels of Flour, all belonging to the Province. Here about 150 Men going towards a Bridge, of which the Enemy were in Possession, the latter fired, and killed 2 of our Men, who then returned the fire, and obliged the Enemy to retreat back to Lexington, where they met Lord Percy, with a large Reinforcement, with two Pieces of Cannon. The Enemy now having a Body of about 1800 Men, made a Halt, picked up many of their Dead, and took Care of their Wounded. At Menotomy, a few of our Men attacked a Party of twelve of the Enemy, (carrying Stores and Provisions to the troops) killed one of them, wounded several, made the Rest Prisoners, and took Possession of all their Arms, Stores, Provisions, etc. without any Loss on our Side. — The Enemy having halted one or two Hours at Lexington, found it necessary to make a second Retreat, carrying with them many of their Dead and Wounded, who they put into Chaises and on Horses that they found standing in the Road. They continued their Retreat from Lexington to Charlestown with great Precipitation; and notwithstanding their Field Pieces, our People continued the Pursuit, firing at them till they got to Charlestown Neck, (which they reached a little after Sunset) over which the Enemy passed, proceeded up Bunker's Hill, and from afterwards went into the Town, under the Protection of the Somerset Man of War of 64 Guns.

In Lexington the Enemy set fire to Deacon Joseph Loring's House and Barn, Mrs. Mulliken's House and Shop, and Mr. Joshua Bond's House and Shop, which were all consumed. They also set Fire to several other Houses, but our People extinguished the Flames. They pillaged almost every House they passed by, breaking and destroying Doors, Windows, Glasses, etc. and carrying off Cloathing and other valuable Effects. It appeared to be their Design to burn and destroy all before them; and nothing but our vigorous Pursuit prevented their internal Purposes from being put in Execution. But the savage Barbarity exercised upon the Bodies of our unfortunate Brethren who fell, is almost incredible: Not content with shooting down the unarmed, aged and infirm, they disregarded the Cries of the wounded, killing them without Mercy, and mangling their Bodies in the most shocking Manner.

We have the Pleasure to Say, that, notwithstanding the highest Provocations, given by the Enemy, not one Instance of Cruelty, that we have heard of, was committed by our victorious Militia; but listening to the merciful Dictates of the Christian Religion, they "breathed higher Sentiments of Humanity."

The Consternation of the people of Charlestown, when our Enemies were entering the Town, is inexpressable; the Troops however behaved tolerably civil, and the people have since nearly all left the town. . . .

Our late Brethren of Danvers, who fell fighting for their Country, were interred, with great Solemnity and respect, on Friday last.

The Public most sincerely sympathize with the Friends and Relations of our deceased Brethren, who gloriously sacrificed their Lives in fighting for the Liberties of their Country. By their noble, intrepid Conduct, in helping to defeat the Forces of an ungrateful Tyrant, they have endeared their Memories to the present Generation, who will transmit their Names to Posterity with the highest Honour.

from

the London Gazette

Whitehall, June 10. Lieutenant Nunn, of the Navy, arrived this morning at Lord Dartmouth's office, and has brought letters from General Gage, Lord Percy, and Lieutenant Colonel Smith, containing the following particulars of what passed on the 19th of April last, between a detachment of the King's troops in the province of Massachusett's Bay, and several parties of Rebel Provincials, viz.

General Gage having received intelligence of a large quantity of military stores being collected at Concord, for the avowed purpose of supplying a body of troops to act in opposition to his Majesty's government, detached, on the 18th of April, at night, the Grenadiers of his army, and the Light Infantry, under the command of Lieutenant Colonel Smith of the 10th regiment, and Major Pitcairne of the Marines, with orders to destroy the said stores; and the next morning eight companies of the 4th, the same number of the 23rd and 49th, and some Marines, marched under the command of Lord Percy, to support the other detachment.

Lieutenant Colonel Smith finding, after he had advanced some miles on his march, that the country had been alarmed by the firing of guns, and ringing of bells, dispatched six companies of Light Infantry, in order to secure two bridges on different roads beyond Concord, who, upon their arrival at Lexington, found a body of the country people drawn up under arms on a green, close to the road; and, upon the King's troops marching up to them, in order to inquire the reason of their being so assembled, they went off in great confusion, and several guns were fired upon the King's troops from behind a stone wall, and also from the Meeting-house and other houses, by which one man was wounded, and Major Pitcairne's horse shot in two places. In consequence of this attack by the rebels, the troops returned the fire, and killed several of them; after which the detachment marched on to Concord, without any thing further happening, where they effected the purpose for which they were

trunnions: pins or pivots on which cannons are swiveled

ordnance: cannon, artillery

intrepidity: bravery

sent, having knocked off the trunnions of three pieces of iron ordnance, burnt some new gun carriages, and a great number of carriage wheels, and thrown into the river a considerable quantity of flour, gunpowder, musket-balls, and other articles. Whilst this service was performing, great numbers of the rebels assembled in many parts, and a considerable body of them attacked the Light Infantry posted on one of the bridges, on which an action ensued, and some few were killed and wounded.

On the return of the troops from Concord they were very much annoyed, and had several men killed and wounded, by the rebels firing from behind walls, ditches, trees, and other ambushes; but the brigade under the command of Lord Percy having joined them at Lexington, with two pieces of cannon, the rebels were for a while dispersed: but, as soon as the troops resumed their march, they began again to fire upon them from behind stone walls and houses, and kept up in that manner a scattering fire, during the whole of their march of fifteen miles, by which means several were killed and wounded. . . .

It is not known what number of the rebels were killed and wounded; but, it is supposed, that their loss was very considerable.

General Gage says, that too much praise cannot be given to Lord Percy, for his remarkable activity during the whole day: and that Lieut. Colonel Smith and Major Pitcairne did every thing that men could do, as did all the officers in general; and that the men behaved with their usual intrepidity.

Discussion Questions

1. **What are some things the articles have in common? What are some things that are different?**
2. **How did personal opinions or interests influence what was recorded?**

from

A Narrative of a Revolutionary Soldier

by Joseph Plumb Martin

Private Martin is the soldier quoted on p. 304 about eating rock-hard wheat cakes at Valley Forge in December, 1776. Here he describes the Battle of Monmouth, 1778.

As soon as the troops had left this ground the British planted their cannon upon the place and began a violent attack upon the artillery and our detachment, but neither could be routed. The cannonade continued for some time without intermission, when the British pieces being mostly disabled, they reluctantly crawled back from the height which they had occupied and hid themselves from our sight.

Before the cannonade had commenced, a part of the right wing of the British army had advanced across a low meadow and brook and occupied an orchard on our left. The weather was almost too hot to live in, and the British troops in the orchard were forced by the heat to shelter themselves from it under the trees. . . . After the British artillery had fallen back and the cannonade had mostly ceased in this quarter, and our detachment had an opportunity to look about us, Colonel (Joseph) Cilly of the New Hampshire Line, who was attached to our detachment, passed along in front of our line, inquiring for General Varnum's men, who were the Connecticut and Rhode Island men belonging to our command. We answered, "Here we are." . . . "Ah!" said he, "you are the boys I want to assist in driving those rascals from yon orchard."

We were immediately ordered from our old detachment and joined another, the whole composing a corps of about five hundred men. We instantly marched towards the enemy's right wing, which was in the orchard, and kept concealed from them as long as possible by keeping behind the bushes. When we could no longer keep ourselves concealed, we marched into the open fields and formed our line. The British immediately formed and began to retreat to the main body of their army.

Discussion Question

Do you think this book was meant to be public or private? What makes you think so?

A Letter from

Abigail Adams

Abigail Adams and her husband, patriot and future president John Adams, wrote many letters to each other when they were apart. As you will hear in this letter, Abigail was not afraid to express her opinions.

vassal: a person who serves a lord

Braintree March 31 1776

I wish you would ever write me a Letter half as long as I write you; and tell me if you may where your Fleet are gone? What sort of Defense Virginia can make against our common Enemy? Whether it is so situated as to make an able Defence? Are not the Genetry Lords and the common people vassals, are they not like the uncivilized Natives Brittain represents us to be? I hope their Riffle Men who have shewen themselves very savage and even Blood thirsty; are not a specimen of the Generality of the people.

I am willing to allow the Colony great merrit for having produced a Washington but they have been shamefully duped by a Dunmore.

I have sometimes been ready to think that the passion for Liberty cannot be Eaquelly Strong in the Breasts of those who have been accustomed to deprive their fellow Creatures of theirs. Of this I am certain that it is not founded upon that generous and christian principal of doing to others as we would that others should do unto us.

Do not you want to see Boston; I am fearfull of the small pox, or I should have been in before this time. I got Mr. Crane to go to our House and see what state it was in. I find it has been occupied by one of the Doctors of a Regiment, very dirty, but no other damage has been done to it. The few things which were left in it are all gone. Cranch has the key which he never delivered up. I have wrote to him for it and am determined to get it cleand as soon as possible and shut it up. I look upon it a new acquisition of property, a property which one month ago I did not value at a single Shilling, and could with pleasure have seen it in flames.

The Town in General is left in a better state than we expected, more oweing to a percipitate flight than any Regard to the inhabitants, tho some individuals discovered a sense of honour and justice and have left the rent of the Houses in which they were, for the owners and the furniture unhurt, or if damaged sufficent to make it good.

Others have committed abominable Ravages. The Mansion House of your President is safe and the furniture unhurt whilst both the House and Furniture of the Solisiter General have fallen a prey to their own merciless party. Surely the very Fiends feel a Reverential awe for Virtue and patriotism, whilst they Detest the paricide and traitor.

I feel very differently at the approach of spring to what I did a month ago. We knew not then whether we could plant or sow with safety, whether when we had toild we could reap the fruits of our own industery, whether we could rest in our own Cottages, or whether we should not be driven from the sea coasts to seek shelter in the wilderness, but now we feel as if we might sit under our own vine and eat the good of the land.

I feel a gaieti de Coar to which before I was a stranger. I think the Sun looks brighter, the Birds sing more melodiously, and Nature puts on a more cheerfull countanance. We feel a temporary peace, and the poor fugitives are returning to their deserted habitations.

Tho we felicitate ourselves, we sympathize with those who are trembling least the Lot of Boston should be theirs. But they cannot be in similar circumstances unless pusilanimity and cowardise should take possession of them. They have time and warning given them to see the Evil and shun it.—I long to hear that you have declared an independency—and by the way in the new Code of Laws which I suppose it will be necessary for you to make I desire you would Remember the Ladies, and be more generous and favorable to them than your ancestors. Do not put such unlimited power into the hands of the Husbands. Remember all Men would be tyrants if they could. If perticuliar care and attention is not paid to the Ladies we are determined to foment a Rebellion, and will not hold ourselves bound by any Laws in which we have no voice, or Representation.

That your Sex are Naturally Tyrannical is a Truth so thoroughly established as to admit of no dispute, but such of you as wish to be happy willingly give up the harsh title of Master for the more tender and endearing one of Friend. Why then, not put it out of the power of the vicious and the Lawless to use us with cruelty and indignity with impunity. Men of Sense in all Ages abhor those customs which treat us only as the vassals of your Sex. Regard us then as Beings placed by providence under your protection and in immitation of the Supreem Being make use of that power only for our happiness.

gaieti de Coar: (French) cheerfulnees

pusilanimity: cowardliness

tyrannical: unjustly powerful

abhor: hate intensely

Discussion Questions

1. **What are some of Abigail Adams' concerns? Do you think many women of her time were concerned with these things?**
2. **What does Abigail have to say about how women are treated?**

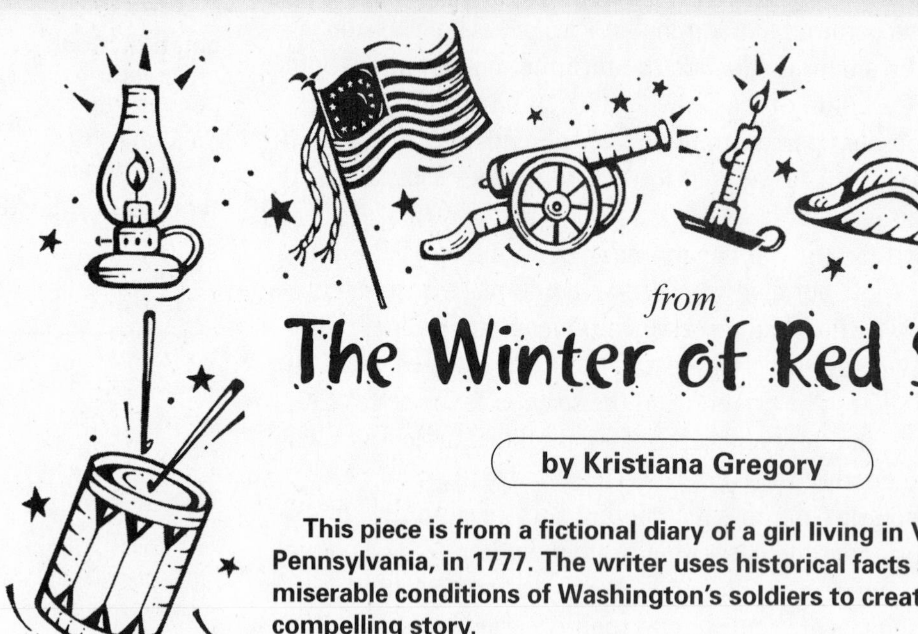

from

The Winter of Red Snow

by Kristiana Gregory

This piece is from a fictional diary of a girl living in Valley Forge, Pennsylvania, in 1777. The writer uses historical facts about the miserable conditions of Washington's soldiers to create a compelling story.

fife: a kind of flute

December 19, 1777, Friday

I woke to sleet hitting the window and another sound I'd not heard before.

A drumbeat.

Papa came in from milking and said, "The soldiers are coming."

Elisabeth, Sally, and I hurriedly ate our porridge, then wrapped ourselves in our cloaks and scarves. Mama watched from the window as we ran into the road. There on the wind from the south came the drumbeat, several drums now and the high trilling of fifes.

"I want to go see the soldiers," Sally said. But Papa said we must stay by our fence.

"It's too cold," he said, as big flakes of snow began to fall. The fields were turning white and the road looked like frosting with chocolate showing through.

Twice we went inside to warm ourselves, for the wind cut through our clothes. Finally through the gray we saw them. Three officers on horseback led. We ran outside to cheer, but the men were quiet and thin. The sight of them took my breath away.

"They have no shoes," Elisabeth whispered.

We watched for several minutes as they passed by.

We were unable to speak.

Their footprints left blood in the snow.

Discussion Question

What parts of this fictional diary entry do you think are true, and what parts do you think the author made up for the story?

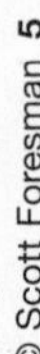

To His Excellency General Washington

by Phillis Wheatley

Phillis Wheatley expressed powerful emotions in this letter and excerpt of a poem to General George Washington. Listen for the rich images that appear in the poem.

Generalissimo: commander in chief of all the armies

Columbia: the female symbol of the United States

Gallic: French

anon: in a while

SIR,

I Have taken the freedom to address your Excellency in the enclosed poem, and retreat your acceptance, though I am not insensible of its inaccuracies. Your being appointed by the Grand Continental Congress to be Generalissimo of the armies of North America, together with the fame of your virtues, excite sensations not easy to suppress. Your generosity, therefore, I presume, will pardon the attempt. Wishing your Excellency all possible success in the great cause you are so generously engaged in. I am,

Your Excellency's most obedient humble servant, PHILLIS WHEATLEY. P*rovidence, Oct. 26, 1775.*

Thee, first in place and honours,—we demand
The grace and glory of thy martial band.
Fam'd for thy valour, for thy virtues more,
Hear every tongue thy guardian aid implore!
One century scarce perform'd its destin'd round,
When Gallic powers Columbia's fury found;
And so may you, whoever dares disgrace
The land of freedom's heaven-defended race!
Fix'd are the eyes of nations on the scales,
For in their hopes Columbia's arm prevails.
Anon Britannia droops the pensive head,
While round increase the rising hills of dead.
Ah! Cruel blindness to Columbia's state!
Lament thy thirst of boundless power too late.
Proceed, great chief, with virtue on thy side,
Thy ev'ry action let the goddess guide.
A crown, a mansion, and a throne that shine,
With gold unfading, WASHINGTON! Be thine.

Discussion Questions

1. **Do you think the letter and poem were meant to be public or private? What makes you think so?**
2. **How do you think Phillis Wheatley felt about Washington?**

from

George Washington's Letter to James Madison

In this letter sent to James Madison, another strong nationalist, on November 5, 1786, George Washington is upset because New England farmers, like Daniel Shays, are calling for changes in land distribution and forgiveness of their personal debts as a reward for winning the colonies from Britain.

superstructure: a structure on top of a structure
verging: tending
replete: full
temper and designs: attitude and plans
annihilate: destroy
Agrarian Laws: laws for distributing land equitably among citizens
supineness: lying down face up

My dear Sir,

. . . Without some alteration in our political creed, the superstructure we have been seven years raising at the expence of much blood and treasure, must fall. We are fast verging to anarchy & confusion! A letter which I have just received from Genl Knox, who had just returned from Massachusetts (whither he had been sent by congress consequent of the commotion in that State) is replete with melancholy information of the temper & designs of a considerable part of that people. among other things he says, "there creed is, that the property of the United States, has been protected from confiscation of Britain by the joint exertion of *all*, and therefore ought to be the *common property* of all. And he that attempts opposition to this creed is an enemy to equity & justice, & ought to be swept from off the face of the Earth." again "They are determined to annihilate all debts public & private, and have Agrarian Laws, which are easily effected by the means of unfunded paper money which shall be a tender in all cases whatever." He adds. "The numbers of these people amount in Massachusetts to about one fifth part of several populous Counties, and to them may be collected, people of similar sentiments from the States of Rhode Island, Connecticut, & New Hampsh[ire] so as to constitute a body of twelve or fifteen thousand desperate, and unprincipled men. They are chiefly of the young & active part of the Commun[ity].

How melancholy is the reflection that in so short a space, we should have made such large strides towards fulfill[ing] the prediction of our transatlantic foes!—"leave them to themselves, and their government will soon dissolve." Will not the wise & good strive hard to avert this evil? Or will their supineness suffer ignorance, and the arts of selfinterested designing disaffected & desperate characters, to involve this rising empire in wretchedness & contempt? What stronger evidence can be given of the want of energy in our governments than these disorders? If there exists not a power to check them, what security has a man of life, liberty, or property? To you, I am sure I need not add aught on this subject, the consequences of a lax, or inefficient government, are too obvious to be dwelt on. Thirteen Sovereignties pulling against each other, and all tugging at the federal head, will soon bring ruin on the whole; whereas a liberal, and energetic Constitution, well guarded & closely watched, to prevent incroachments, might restore us to that degree of respectability & consequence, to which we had a fair claim, & the brightest prospect of attaining—With sentiments of the sincerest esteem & regard I am—Dear Sir Yr Most Obedt & Affecte Hble Servt

Go: Washington

aught: anything

encroachments: trespasses

Discussion Questions

1. **Why do you think the government in 1786 could not control "disorders" like those in New England?**
2. **Would you have agreed with Washington that something was necessary to protect "life, liberty, and property"? What solution would you have favored?**

Speech at the Close of the Constitutional Convention

by Benjamin Franklin

Benjamin Franklin gave this persuasive speech to his fellow delegates on September 9, 1787, just before the vote on the Constitution. In it, his humor and his doubts about government are evident.

doctrine: set of principles
infallible: incapable of error
despotism: dictatorship
despotic: dictatorial

Mr. President,

I confess, that I do not entirely approve of this Constitution at present; but, Sir, I am not sure I shall never approve it; for, having lived long, I have experienced many instances of being obliged, by better information or fuller consideration, to change my opinions even on important subjects, which I once thought right, but found to be otherwise. It is therefore that, the older I grow, the more apt I am to doubt my own judgement of others. Most men, indeed, as well as most sects in religion, think themselves in possession of all truth, and wherever others differ from them, it is so far error. Steele, a Protestant, in a dedication, tells the Pope, that the only difference between our two churches in their opinions of the certainty of their doctrine, is, the Romish Church is *infallible*, and the Church of England is *never in the wrong*. But, though many private Persons think almost as highly of their own infallibility as of that of their Sect, few express it so naturally as a certain French Lady, who, in a little dispute with her sister, said, "But I meet with nobody but myself that is *always* in the right." *"Je ne trouve que moi qui aie toujours raison."*

In these moments, Sir, I agree to this Constitution, with all its faults,—if they are such; because I think a general Government necessary for us, and there is no *form* of government but what may be a blessing to the people, if well administered; and I believe, farther, that this is likely to be well administered for a course of years, and can only end in despotism, as other forms have done before it, when the people shall become so corrupted as to need despotic government, being incapable of any other. I doubt too, whether any other Convention we can obtain, may be able to make a better Constitution; for, when you assemble a number of men, to have the advantage of their joint wisdom, you inevitably assemble with those men all their prejudices, their passions, their errors of opinion, their local interests, and their selfish views. From such an assembly can a *perfect* production be expected? It therefore astonishes me, Sir, to find this system approaching so near to perfection as it does; and I think it will astonish our enemies, who are waiting with confidence to hear, that our councils are confounded like those of the Builders of Babel, and that our States are on the point of separation, only to meet hereafter for the purpose of cutting one another's throats. Thus I consent, Sir, to this Constitution, because I expect no better, and because I am not sure that it is the best. The opinions I have had of its errors I sacrifice to the public good. I have never whispered a syllable of them abroad. Within these walls they were born, and here shall they die. If every one of us, in returning to our Constituents, were to report the objections he has had to it, and endeavor to gain Partisans in support of them, we might prevent its being generally received, and thereby lose all the salutary effects and great advantages resulting naturally in our favour among foreign nations, as well as among ourselves, from our real or apparent unanimity. Much of the strength and efficiency of any government, in procuring and securing happiness to the people, depends on *opinion*, on the general opinion of the goodness of that government, as well as of the wisdom and integrity of its governors. I hope, therefore, for our own sakes, as a part of the people, and for the sake of our posterity, that we shall act heartily and unanimously in recommending this Constitution, thoughts and endeavors to the means of having it *well administered.*

On the whole, Sir, I cannot help expressing a wish, that every member of the Convention who may still have objections to it, would with me on this occasion doubt a little of his own infallibility, and, to make *manifest* our *unanimity*, put his name to this Instrument.

confounded . . . Builders of Babel: defeated like the people in the Bible who tried to build a tower to heaven and were prevented by God having them speak many different languages

constituents: voters or people requesting representation

partisans: supporters of one side of a debate

put his name to this Instrument: sign the Constitution

Discussion Questions

1. **If you had been a delegate to the convention, how would you have reacted to Franklin's speech?**
2. **Why do you think Franklin doesn't "entirely approve of this Constitution" but will sign it and wants everyone else to sign it too?**

George Washington's Address to Congress

In this speech, given November 19, 1794, George Washington describes what occurred in Pennsylvania when some people rioted against the 1790 excise tax. Not knowing how big the rebellion would be, Washington sent 15,000 men to control the uprising.

insurrection: rebellion
lament: be sad
diverted to a new application: used up for new purposes
not wanting: not lacking
vigilance: watchfulness
clime: region
fomented: stirred up
disseminated: spread
deputed: authorized

When we call to mind the gracious indulgence of Heaven, by which the American People became a nation; when we survey the general prosperity of our country, and look forward to the riches, power, and happiness, to which it seems destined; with the deepest regret do I announce to you, that during your recess, some of the citizens of the United States have been found capable of an insurrection. . . .

While there is cause to lament, that occurrences of this nature should have disgraced the name, or interrupted the tranquillity of any part of our community, or should have diverted to a new application, any portion of the public resources, there are not wanting real and substantial consolations for the misfortune. It has demonstrated, that our prosperity rests on solid foundations; by furnishing an additional proof, that my fellow citizens understand the true principles of government and liberty: that they feel their inseparable union. . . .

To every description, indeed, of citizens let praise be given. But let them presevere in their affectionate vigilance over that precious depository of American happiness, the constitution of the United States. Let them cherish it too, for the sake of those, who from every clime are daily seeking a dwelling in our land. And when in the calm moments of reflection, they shall have retraced the origin and progress of the insurrection, let them determine, whether it has not been fomented by combinations of men, who . . . have disseminated, from an ignorance or version of facts, suspicions, jealousies, and accusations of the whole government.

Having thus fulfilled the engagement, which I took . . . "to the best of my ability to preserve, protect, and defend the constitution of the United States," on you, Gentlemen, and the people by whom you are deputed, I rely for support.

Discussion Questions

1. **How do you think the uprising showed that "citizens understand the true principles of government and liberty"?**
2. **Why do you think the U.S. president's oath of office says to preserve, protect, and "defend the constitution of the United States" rather than just "defend the United States"?**

A Letter from

Benjamin Banneker to Thomas Jefferson

This is part of the letter that Benjamin Banneker sent to Secretary of State Thomas Jefferson. In it, Banneker asks that Jefferson use his influence to convince other leaders that all people are equal, regardless of their color or situation.

Sir,

I am fully sensible of the greatness of that freedom, which I take with you on the present occasion; a liberty which seemed to me scarcely allowable, when I reflected on that distinguished and dignified station in which you stand, and the almost general prejudice and prepossession, which is so prevalent in the world against those of my complexion.

I suppose it is a truth too well attested to you, to need a proof here, that we are a race of beings, who have long labored under the abuse and censure of the world; that we have long been looked upon with an eye of contempt; and that we have long been considered rather as brutish than human, and scarcely capable of mental endowments.

Sir, I hope I may safely admit, in consequence of that report which hath reached me, that you are a man far less inflexible in sentiments of this nature, than many others; that you are measurably friendly, and well disposed towards us; and that you are willing and ready to lend your aid and assistance to our relief, from those many distresses, and numerous calamities, to which we are reduced. Now Sir, if this is founded in truth, I apprehend you will embrace every opportunity, to eradicate that train of absurd and false ideas and opinions, which so generally prevails with respect to us; and that your sentiments are concurrent with mine, which are, that one universal Father hath given being to us all; and that he hath not only made us all of one flesh, but that he hath also, without partiality, afforded us all the same sensations and endowed us all with the same faculties; and that however variable we may be in society or religion, however diversified in situation or color, we are all of the same family, and stand in the same relation to him.

prepossession: attitude formed beforehand
attested: stated
censure: judgment, criticism
apprehend: understand
eradicate: remove
concurrent: in agreement
faculties: abilities

Discussion Questions

1. **How do you think Jefferson would have responded to this letter? Why?**
2. **Have you ever written a letter to someone you didn't know to try to persuade him or her to do something? What happened?**

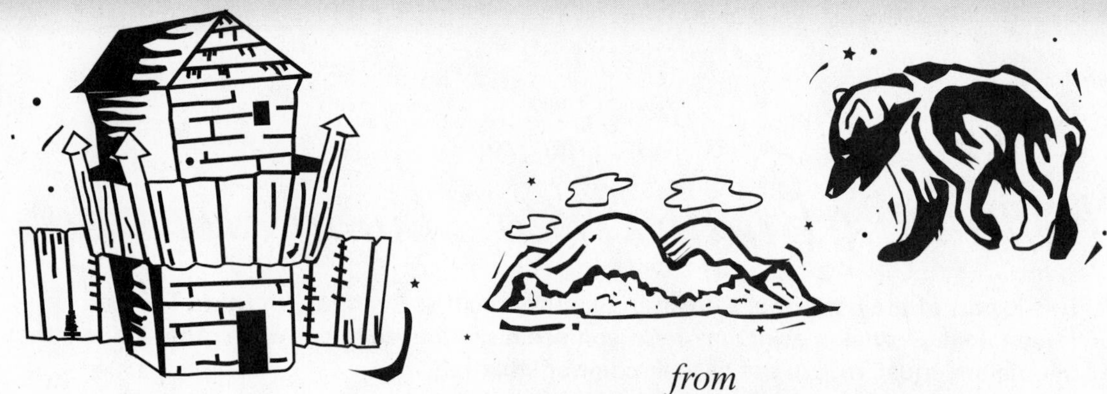

from

Daniel Boone: The Opening of the Wilderness

by John Mason Brown

This chapter begins with the long-awaited arrival of Daniel's wife, Rebecca, and children at the Boonesborough, Kentucky, settlement. Richard Henderson, owner of the Transylvania Company, has financed this and other Kentucky settlements and, having traded goods to the Cherokee for 20 million acres of land, has a shaky title to the ground on which the Boones have staked their futures.

It is not hard to guess what the men who had built those cabins thought when they saw Rebecca and Daniel's family coming to join them. A place fit for women and children was no longer a camp. It was a settlement, a real settlement, meant to last—the beginning of a town.

In no time other families followed. Squire Boone brought his. The Calloways came with their two daughters. The secret door in the mountains had been pried open; the westward movement had begun in earnest. By the end of the first year more wives had arrived with their growing sons and daughters.

Boonesborough was not the only goal of the men, women, and children who traveled over the Wilderness Road or came down the Ohio. There were by now three other settlements within the lands Henderson had purchased. There was the outpost, or "station," which Benjamin Logan had built to the south at St. Asaph. There was another small station at Boiling Spring. Largest and oldest was Harrodsburg, some fifty miles to the west of Boonesborough. James Harrod had laid it out the year before, and had returned to it with a hundred men at the end of Lord Dunmore's War.

The people in these three settlements had no liking for Henderson's Transylvania Company or the kind of government he wanted to set up. They doubted if his treaty with the Cherokees really entitled him to the vast tract he claimed as his. Since they had reached it first, and built on it, they thought the land was theirs. The fact that there were more of them than there were of Henderson's followers gave them a feeling of strength which added to their sense of being right. This did not make things easy or comfortable for Henderson.

In the next few years other settlements would be started in Kentucky within and far beyond Transylvania. Some of these were to be abandoned during the coming war. Several were to take root. All were to face the terror of Indian attacks. Most of the men and women who came—and had the hardihood to stay—were of Scotch-Irish stock. They were a resolute group. . . .

Among them were some who became national heroes. One of these was the famous scout and Indian fighter Simon Kenton, whose bravery and quick-wittedness can be measured by what he did one April day in 1778 to save Daniel's life. When the Shawnees were attacking Boonesborough, as they were fond of doing, he and Daniel had gone out with a party and been ambushed. Daniel had fallen to the ground, his ankle shattered. . . . Kenton . . . made a dash for the fort carrying Daniel on his back.

Among these early settlers was George Rogers Clark, that brave and colorful figure who was to emerge during the Revolution as America's outstanding military leader on the frontier. He, too, knew Daniel and in the coming years would get to know him better under the tests of battle.

It was Clark who was to organize a militia in Kentucky. It was he who was to carry the war into the enemy-held territories to the north and seize the English forts on the Mississippi at Cahokia and Kaskaskia. Above all, it was he who was to take Fort Vincennes, and then retake it by a brilliant march across swamps in icy weather, forcing its redcoated garrison to surrender in February, 1779. It was he who captured there Henry Hamilton, the British lieutenant-governor. . . .

If at the time of Rebecca's arrival at Boonesborough people were on the move, so were events, and far more swiftly. When the storm of the American Revolution broke, it struck Kentucky as hard as it did the seaboard. No cabin door could be shut against the gale; no stockade was safe from its fury. The British under Hamilton made certain of this. Needing allies, they did everything they could to stir up the Indians against the Americans and send them on the warpath once more.

When this happened and the massacres in the wilderness began to multiply, many settlers were frightened. . . . These weaker ones hurried back across the mountains, leaving only the iron-willed behind.

During one desperate winter the number of people in Kentucky dwindled to a mere two hundred. The importance to the American fight for independence of this small group, and of those who came to reinforce them, cannot be overestimated. They formed a line of defense which kept the back door to the southern colonies closed on Indians and British alike.

Henderson's plans did not escape the storm. Its lightning put a quick end to his Transylvania Company. Shortly after his arrival at Boonesborough, Henderson held a congress near the cabins under a great elm. His hope was to establish a government—*his* government—at this meeting and to win men like Harrod and Logan to his side. Among the speakers was Daniel. As might be expected, he did not discuss law or politics. He urged that a bill be passed to preserve game. . . .

Although Henderson tried to gain the support of the Continental Congress and the Virginia Legislature, neither of these bodies approved of his Transylvania project. They knew the military value of the lands to the west. They knew the British had forts in Detroit and along the Mississippi. They knew the English would have little trouble persuading the Indians to go to war. They knew a militia was needed to defend the frontier, and that men fighting for freedom would not fight for a colony largely owned and run by one man.

The arguments they listened to were the very sensible ones of such men as Harrod and George Rogers Clark who, for the safety of all concerned, asked that Kentucky be made a county of Virginia.

This action was taken. Kentucky County was formed, and two years later the Transylvania Company was declared illegal. The valuable work Henderson and his partners had done in opening up her new county was not forgotten, however, by Virginia. As thanks they were granted two hundred thousand acres in Kentucky.

Henderson had intended, after the cutting of the Wilderness Road and the founding of Boonesborough, to express his gratitude to Daniel by giving him two thousand acres. But, in the process of Kentucky's becoming a part of Virginia and the Transylvania Company's being put out of business, Daniel never received his present. Although he was disappointed, the long fierce struggle of the Revolution left him little time to grieve over the reward that should have been his.

Discussion Questions

1. **If you had been a settler in Kentucky, what personal qualities would have helped you stay and survive?**
2. **Do you think it would have been a good thing for Henderson to establish his own government in Kentucky? Why or why not?**

from

The Journals of Meriwether Lewis and William Clark

In these excerpts from their journals, Meriwether Lewis and William Clark describe events that took place as they approached the Rockies on their journey westward.

embarked: got onto a boat
radical: basic

April 22, 1805
Meriwether Lewis

walking on shore this evening I met with a buffaloe calf which attatched itself to me and continued to follow close at my heels untill I embarked and left it. it appeared allarmed at my dog which was probably the cause of it's so readily attaching itself to me.

April 24, 1805
Meriwether Lewis

The wind blew so hard during the whole of this day, that we were unable to move. . . . Soar eyes is a common complaint among the party. I believe it origenates from the immence quantities of sand which is driven by the wind from the sandbars of the river in such clouds that you are unable to discover the opposite bank of the river in many instances. . . . so penitrating is this sand that we cannot keep any article free from it; in short we are compelled to eat, drink, and breath it very freely. my pocket watch, is out of order, she will run only a few minutes without stoping. I can discover no radical defect in her works, and must therefore attribute it to the sand, with which, she seems plentifully charged, notwithstanding her cases are double and tight.

April 25, 1805
Meriwether Lewis

The buffaloe Elk and Antelope are so gentle that we pass near them while feeding, without appearing to excite any alarm among them; and when we attract their attention, they frequently approach us more nearly to discover what we are, and in some instances pursue us a considerable distance apparently with that view.

lome: loam; rich, fertile soil

Squar: squaw; Indian woman (the Shoshone guide, Sacagawea)

April 27, 1805
Meriwether Lewis

. . . altho' game is very abundant and gentle, we only kill as much as is necessary for food. I believe that two good hunters could conveniently supply a regiment with provisions.

May 01, 1805
Meriwether Lewis

. . . the country appears much more pleasant and fertile than that we have passed for several days; the hills are lower, the bottoms wider, and better stocked with timber, which consists principally of cottonwood, not however of large size; the under-growth willow on the verge of the river and sandbars, rose bushes, red willow and the broad leafed willow in the bottom lands; the high country on either side of the river is one vast plain, intirely destitute of timber, but is apparently fertile, consisting of a dark rich mellow looking lome.

May 02, 1805
Meriwether Lewis

. . . snow . . . being about one inch deep, . . . the flesh of the beaver is esteemed a delecacy among us; I think the tale a most delicious morsal, when boiled it resembles in flavor the fresh tongues and sounds of the codfish, and is usually sufficiently large to afford a plentifull meal for two men.

May 04, 1805
Meriwether Lewis

I saw immence quantities of buffaloe in every direction, also some Elk deer and goats; having an abundance of meat on hand I passed them without firing on them; they are extremely gentle the bull buffaloe particularly will scarcely give way to you. I passed several in the open plain within fifty paces, they viewed me for a moment as something novel and then very unconcernedly continued to feed.

May 08, 1805
Meriwether Lewis

The water of this river possesses a peculiar whiteness, being about the color of a cup of tea with the admixture of a tablespoonfull of milk. from the color of it's water we called it Milk river.

May 08, 1805
William Clark

. . . the Squar Geathered on the sides of the hills wild Lickerish, & the white apple . . . and gave me to eat, . . .

May 09, 1805
Meriwether Lewis

This stream (if such it can properly be termed) we called Big dry river. . . . Charbono calls the boudin (poudingue) blanc, . . . this white pudding we all esteem one of the greatest del[ic]acies of the forrest. . . .

we saw a great quantity of game today particularly of Elk and Buffaloe, the latter are now so gentle that the men frequently throw sticks and stones at them in order to drive them out of the way. . . . the river for several days has been as wide as it is generally near it's mouth, tho' it is much shallower or I should begin to despair of ever reaching it's source; . . . the water also appears to become clearer, it has changed it's complexin very considerably. I begin to feel extreemly anxious to get in view of the rocky mountains.

Charbono: French trapper, husband of Sacagawea and father of her son

May 11, 1805
Meriwether Lewis

About 5 P.M. my attention was struck by one of the party running at a distance towards us and making signs and hollowing as if in distress, . . . I now found that it was Bratton. . . . at length he informed me . . . below us he had shot a brown bear which immediately turned on him and pursued him a considerable distance but he had wounded it so badly that it could not overtake him; . . . it was a monstrous beast, not quite so large as that we killed a few days past but in all other rispects much the same. . . . we now found that Bratton had shot him through the center of the lungs, notwithstanding which he had pursued him near half a mile and had returned more than double that distance and with his tallons had prepared himself a bed in the earth of about 2 feet deep and five long and was perfectly alive when we found him which could not have been less than 2 hours after he received the wound; these bear being so hard to die rather intimedates us all; I must confess that I do not like the gentlemen and had reather fight two Indians than one bear.

May 12, 1805
Meriwether Lewis

(Re: bears)

. . . I have therefore come to a resolution to act on the defencive only, should I meet these gentlemen in the open country.

Perogue: dugout canoe

obliquely: at a slant

lufted . . . it: turned the boat so the sail faced the oncoming wind

righted: became upright

gunwales: upper edges of the boat's sides

May 14, 1805
Meriwether Lewis

. . . the bear pursued and had very nearly overtaken them before they reached the river; . . . in this manner he pursued two of them separately so close that they were obliged to throw aside their guns and pouches and throw themselves into the river altho' the bank was nearly twenty feet perpendicular; so enraged was this anamal that he plunged into the river only a few feet behind the second man he had compelled [to] take refuge in the water, when one of those who still remained on shore shot him . . . and finally killed him; . . . It happened unfortunately for us this evening that Charbono was at the helm of this Perogue, in stead of Drewyer, who had previously steered her; Charbono cannot swim and is perhaps the most timid waterman in the world; . . . in short almost every article indispensibly necessary to further the views, or insure the success of the enterprise in which we are now launched . . . when a sudon squawl of wind struck her obliquely, and turned her considerably, the steersman allarmed, in stead of puting, her before the wind, lufted her up into it, the wind was so violent that it drew the brace of the squarsail out of the hand of the man who was attending it, and instantly upset the perogue and would have turned her completely topsaturva, had it not have been from the resistance mad[e] by the oarning against the water; . . . the perogue then wrighted but had filled within an inch of the gunwals; Charbono still crying to his god for mercy, had not yet recollected the rudder, nor could the repeated orders of the Bowsman, Cruzat, bring him to his recollection untill he threatend to shoot him instantly if he did not take hold of the rudder and do his duty, . . . had I undertaken this project therefore, there was a hundred to one but what I should have paid the forfit of my life for the madness of my project, but this had the perogue been lost, I should have valued but little.

May 14, 1805
William Clark

. . . the articles which floated out was nearly all caught by the Squar who was in the rear.

Discussion Questions

1. **Why do you think Lewis writes about the behavior of the animals he sees?**
2. **What would you like most about being on an expedition like this? What would you like the least?**

Students might like to read more of Lewis and Clark's journals and trace their path on a map.

from

Streams to the River, River to the Sea: A Novel of Sacagawea

by Scott O'Dell

This excerpt from Scott O'Dell's fictional autobiography of Sacagawea includes a description of Charbonneau mishandling the boat, the same incident that Lewis recorded in his journal.

Every day Captain Clark made black marks in a thing he called a journal. He made the marks with a stick he dipped in black paint. He said the marks were words that told everything he had seen or heard or thought that day.

When I went down to the river, he was there, sitting in one of the big boats. The journal was in his lap. He motioned me to put down the bag and the cradleboard and to sit beside him. He opened the journal, wet the stick, and put it in my hand. He put his arm around my shoulder and took my hand and guided it over the paper.

These are the things that we put in the journal together:

> Fort Mandan April the 7th 1805
> Sunday, at 4 o' Clock PM, the boat, in which were 6 soldiers, 2 Frenchmen and an Indian, all under the command of a corporal who had the charge of dispatches, &c.—and a canoe with 2 Frenchmen, set out down the river for St. Louis. At the same time we set out on our voyage up the river in 2 perogues and 6 canoes.

That was all I wrote while Captain Clark guided my hand. I looked at the marks as they ran back and forth on the page. I felt very proud of myself. Not until much later, when I began to learn more about the white man's language, did I know what all the marks meant.

Captain Clark wrote some more in his journal.

I saw the word "Janey," the name he had given to me. He quickly sprinkled the words with sand to dry them off. I suppose they had something to do with me.

cradleboard: infant carrier used by the Shoshone
dispatches: messages
Mandan: North Dakota tribe

rudder: large flat piece of wood or metal at the stern of a boat used for steering

The big silver boat that looked like a gull went down the river. Captain Lewis fired his swivel guns to say goodbye to the Mandans and we went fast up the river.

Near nightfall everyone waded to shore and I was sent out to dig roots for supper. Both of the big boats, the pirogues, were stored with food, but Captain Clark planned to use it only if nothing could be found on land. I was sent out because Charbonneau had said when the captain hired him that he should have more money because I, his wife, knew how to gather berries and all kinds of roots.

Finding roots was easy. I had done it since I was a child. . . .

It was the end of winter and the mice had eaten most of their store, so I had to dig long after dark. I dug enough roots for more than three dozen men. . . .

Since the men were hungry, I just boiled the roots. I dug them and cooked them because I wanted to please Captain Clark.

Charbonneau was angry. He said to Captain Clark at supper, "Me and wife, Bird Girl, get no pay for cook. For talk. For guide. No cook."

"Janey wanted to dig the roots and cook them," Captain Clark said. "The men usually cook for themselves."

"Good," Charbonneau said. Afterward he said to me, "You no cook. Find roots, no cook. See?"

I was not displeased. To cook for three dozen hungry men was more than I could do.

We passed a Minnetaree village early the next morning, the one Le Borgne ruled over. The river runs narrow here past a low cliff and he was watching for us as we came out of the mist. He raised his hand and pointed at a huge pile of meat on the bank beside him.

"Buffalo," he shouted. "Welcome to good eating. Welcome, friends."

Captain Clark shouted back, but when Charbonneau, who was steering, turned toward shore, Captain Clark grabbed the rudder and kept us headed straight. It was well that he did. For when we floated by and left Le Borgne standing on the bank, a shower of arrows from the cliff fell upon us.

For the first time I wondered about Charbonneau. He had heard the horrible tales about Le Borgne. He knew that the one-eyed chieftain could not be trusted, that he hated the white men. Knowing this, why had Charbonneau tried to steer the boat ashore into the hands of an enemy?

Only a few days later, less than a week, I wondered even more about him. He was at the rudder of our pirogue when a gust of wind struck us and wrested the rudder from his grip. Instead of taking hold of the rudder again, he raised his hands and began to pray.

The other boats were farther up the river.

Cruzatte, the bowsman, shouted at Charbonneau, "Turn her, you fool!" Charbonneau was still praying. Cruzatte shouted again, "Turn her!"

Charbonneau was on his knees, clinging to the pirogue with one hand.

"Turn!" Cruzatte shouted again. "Turn her or I'll shoot you!" . . .

The sails flapped and we tilted. Water rushed in. It swept around my knees. The baby started to cry. I saw that the shore was not far away and that I could reach it. Then I saw that our stores had begun to drift out of the boat. Charbonneau watched them drift but did not move.

Cruzatte seized the rudder.

We were floating with the current now and around us in a wide circle the water was covered with the stores that had drifted out of the boat. I saw Captain Clark's journal and a wooden box that held something he valued. He took it out of the box every day, looked at it, and carefully put it back.

Someone shouted from the shore. Waves were beating so loud against the boat I could not make out what was said, but it had a warning sound. The cradleboard had loosened. I tightened the cord that bound it to my shoulders and let myself into the water. It came up higher than my waist.

The first thing I gathered in was the wooden box. Then I grasped the journal that I had written in once and Captain Clark wrote in almost every day. A wave broke over our heads and the baby began to cry, so I gave up and climbed back in the boat.

I got safely to land but we lost most of our medicine, gunpowder, flour, melon seeds that Captain Clark was going to plant somewhere, and many other things, besides some of our beads and presents for people along the way. But I saved his journal and the wooden box. He was pleased to see them when he came back that night.

"Good as new," he said, opening the box. "I have a small one, but this is by far the best."

"What is it?" I asked him.

"A compass. You can tell whether you are traveling north or south or east or west. Otherwise you get lost. "

He was so pleased that he kissed me on the cheek and gave me a beautiful gift.

wrested: took by force

Discussion Questions

1. **What are some differences between this account of Charbonneau's actions and Lewis's description in his journal?**
2. **In your opinion, what are some advantages of writing a fictional autobiography? What drawbacks might there be?**

from

Jackson's First Annual Message to Congress

In his first annual message to Congress, given in 1829, President Andrew Jackson explains why it would be humane and just to set aside land for the Indian tribes.

propriety: suitability
without: outside
commonwealth: self-governed nation or state
attest: bear witness to
aborigines: original inhabitants of a particular place

Our conduct toward these people is deeply interesting to our national character. . . . Our ancestors found them the uncontrolled possessors of these vast regions. By persuasion and force they have been made to retire from river to river and from mountain to mountain, until some of the tribes have become extinct and others have left but remnants to preserve for awhile their once terrible names. Surrounded by the whites with their arts of civilization, which by destroying the resources of the savage doom him to weakness and decay, the fate of the Mohegan, the Narragansett, and the Delaware is fast overtaking the Choctaw, the Cherokee, and the Creek. . . . Humanity and national honor demand that every effort should be made to avert so great a calamity. . . .

As a means of effecting this end I suggest for your consideration the propriety of setting apart an ample district west of the Mississippi, and without the limits of any State or Territory now formed, to be guaranteed to the Indian tribes as long as they shall occupy it, each tribe having a distinct control over the portion designated for its use. There they may be secured in the enjoyment of governments of their own choice, subject to no other control from the United States than such as may be necessary to preserve peace on the frontier and between the several tribes. There the benevolent may endeavor to teach them the arts of civilization, and, by promoting union and harmony among them, to raise up an interesting commonwealth, destined to perpetuate the race and to attest the humanity and justice of this Government.

This emigration should be voluntary, for it would be as cruel as unjust to compel the aborigines to abandon the graves of their fathers and seek a home in a distant land.

Discussion Questions

1. **Do you think that Jackson's solution was just and humane? Why or why not?**
2. **What did the southeastern tribes have to lose by moving?**

from

The Monroe Doctrine

This excerpt is taken from President James Monroe's seventh annual message to Congress, delivered December 2, 1823. Monroe formally, and very diplomatically, warned the European governments not to try further colonizing the Americas.

The occasion has been judged proper for asserting, as a principle in which the rights and interests of the United States are involved, that the American continents, by the free and independent condition which they have assumed and maintain, are henceforth not to be considered as subjects for future colonization by any European powers. . . .

In the wars of the European powers in matters relating to themselves we have never taken any part, nor does it comport with our policy to do so. It is only when our rights are invaded or seriously menaced that we resent injuries or make preparation for our defense. With the movements in this hemisphere we are of necessity more immediately connected, and by causes which must be obvious to all enlightened and impartial observers. The political system of the allied powers is essentially different in this respect from that of America. This difference proceeds from that which exists in their respective Governments; and to the defense of our own, which has been achieved by the loss of so much blood and treasure, and matured by the wisdom of their most enlightened citizens, and under which we have enjoyed unexampled felicity, this whole nation is devoted. We owe it, therefore, to candor and to the amicable relations existing between the United States and those powers to declare that we should consider any attempt on their part to extend their system to any portion of this hemisphere as dangerous to our peace and safety.

asserting: stating
assumed: taken on
comport: agree
impartial: neutral
allied powers: governments united by agreement
felicity: happiness
candor: honesty

Discussion Questions

1. **Why do you think Monroe speaks for "the American continents" instead of just for the United States?**
2. **Why might Monroe mention that the United States does not take part in European wars?**
3. **What effect do you think Monroe hoped this speech would have?**

from

The Cherokee Removal

by Glen Fleischmann

This passage, containing excerpts from newspaper articles of the period, details the forced relocation of 19,000 Cherokees from their homes in Georgia, Tennessee, Alabama, and North Carolina across 800 miles to Indian Territory.

On May 23, 1838, the United States Army under the command of General Winfield Scott and augmented by militia units from the states of Georgia, Tennessee, Alabama, and North Carolina, to a total strength of 9,494 men, began evicting from their homes 19,000 Cherokee Indians and driving them into stockades. Then, after some unforeseen delays, the Cherokees were removed to lands west of the Mississippi River. In the roundup and in the stockades, and on the journey of over eight hundred miles, 4,000 Cherokees—more than one-fifth of their Nation—died of cholera, dysentery, fever, exposure, improper care of mothers giving birth, and, especially in the aged, loss of the will to survive.

The Cherokees had been living at peace with their neighbors for over two generations. Though some were hunters, trappers, and herb gatherers, they were not warriors or wanderers. Many were planters, tradesmen, herdsmen, craftsmen, artisans, teachers, living in a settled way of life, as they had been advised and encouraged to do, by each successive President of the United States from George Washington to John Quincy Adams. In adapting themselves to an agrarian economy and a settled existence, the Cherokees were succeeding so well that repeatedly they were visited by white people of American cities, and by Europeans, curious to observe what seemed to be a cultural and ethnological phenomenon—a primitive people changing itself into a civilized nation in two generations.

The sudden, forced expulsion of the Cherokees from their homeland was observed with horror by the whole civilized Western world. It was denounced in newspapers in America and in Europe, and in the Congress of the United States. . . .

The route of this emigration, whether starting from Calhoun or Ross's Landing in Tennessee, or Gunter's Landing in Alabama, passed through Nashville, continued northwest through Hopkinsville, Kentucky, crossed the Mississippi River at Cape Girardeau, Missouri, or Green's Ferry, then proceeded southwest to Fort Smith and Fort Gibson, Indian Territory.

After the drought had broken there was plenty of rain.

The *Nashville Banner* reported that roads traveled by the emigrants were in wretched condition, many places axle deep in mud. The last contingent, numbering about 1,800, passed through Nashville on December 2, nearly a month after it had started from Calhoun. Emigrants were suffering much from cold.

The *Arkansas Gazette*, December 20, reported of one contingent that "owing to their exposure to the inclemency of the weather, and many of them being destitute of shoes and other necessary articles of clothing, about 50 of them have died." On January 2 the same newspaper reported on a caravan of 1,200 that passed through Smithville, on December 12: "They have the measles and whooping cough among them and there is an average of four deaths per day."

The *New York Observer*, January 26, 1839, carried an article signed by "A Native of Maine, traveling in the Western Country," which gave this account:

". . . On Tuesday evening we fell in with a detachment of the poor Cherokee, . . about eleven hundred Indians—sixty waggons—six hundred horses, and perhaps forty pairs of oxen. We found them in the forest camped for the night by the roadside, . . . under a severe fall of rain accompanied by heavy wind. With their canvas for a shield from the inclemency of the weather, and the cold wet ground for a resting place, after the fatigue of the day, they spent the night. Many of the aged Indians were suffering extremely from the fatigue of the journey and the ill health consequent upon it, . . . several were then quite ill, and one aged man we were informed was then in the last struggles of death. . . .

"We met several detachments in the southern part of Kentucky on the 4th, 5th and 6th of December. . . . The last detachment we passed on the 7th embraced rising two thousand Indians with horses and mules in proportion. The forward part of the train we found just pitching their tents for the night, and notwithstanding some thirty or forty waggons were already stationed, the road was literally filled with the procession for about three miles. . . . We learned from the inhabitants on the road where the Indians passed, that they buried fourteen and fifteen at every stopping place. . . .

"The Indians as a whole carry in their countenances everything but the appearance of happiness. . . . Most of them seemed intelligent and refined. . . . Some Cherokees are wealthy and travel in style.

"One lady passed on in her hack in company with her husband, apparently with as much refinement and equipage as any mother of New England; and she was a mother too and her youngest child about three years old was sick in her arms, and all she could do was make it comfortable as circumstances would permit. She could only carry her

embraced rising: included almost

countenances: faces

hack: coach for hire

equipage: equipment

consign: turn over
forbear: control myself

dying child in her arms a few miles farther, and then she must stop in a stranger-land and consign her much loved babe to the cold ground, and that too without ceremony, and pass on with the multitude. . . .

"When I passed the last detachment of those suffering exiles and thought that my countrymen had thus expelled them from their native soil and their much loved homes, . . . I turned from the sight with feelings which language cannot express and 'wept like childhood' then. . . .

"When I read in the President's Message that he was happy to inform the Congress that the Cherokees were peaceably and without reluctance removed—and remember that it was on the 4th day of December, when not one of the detachments had reached their destination; and that a large majority had not made even half their journey, I wished the President could have been there that day in Kentucky with myself, and have seen the comfort and the willingness with which the Cherokees were making their journey. But I forbear, full well I know that many prayers have gone up to the King of Heaven from Maine in behalf of the poor Cherokees."

The caravans arrived at Fort Smith, Indian Territory, January 4, 7, 10, February 2, 23, 27, March 1, 2, 5, 14, 18, 24, 25, 1839.

Chief John Ross and his family, with the last party of Cherokees to leave their homeland, arrived at Little Rock, February 1, aboard the steamboat *Victoria*. The party numbered 228, many of whom sickness had prevented from starting on the journey by land. The Ross family were mourning the death of their wife and mother, Elizabeth Brown Henley Ross, known to her friends as "Quatie." She had died as the boat approached Little Rock, and was buried there, in the cemetery lot of a family friend, General Albert Pike.

Discussion Questions

1. **Why were the Cherokees unusual among Native American tribes?**
2. **What do you think the Maine writer means when he says he "wished the President could have been there that day in Kentucky with myself, and have seen the comfort and the willingness with which the Cherokees were making their journey"?**
3. **Do you think the newspaper accounts of the Cherokee removal are valuable? Why or why not?**

from

Early Factory Labor in New England

by Harriet Hanson Robinson

This excerpt is from Harriet Robinson's account of her life as a Lowell mill girl, from age 10 to age 24. She discusses the status of the girls, the reasons they worked, and their first strikes in 1836. The account was published in 1883 in the annual report of the Massachusetts Bureau of Statistics of Labor.

so much a head: fee per individual
caste: social level
opprobrium: disgrace
mites: tiny creatures

In what follows I shall confine myself to a description of factory life in Lowell, Massachusetts, from 1832 to 1848, since, with that phase of Early Factory Labor in New England, I am the most familiar—because I was a part of it.

In 1832, Lowell was little more than a factory village. Five "corporations" were started, and the cotton mills belonging to them were building. Help was in great demand and stories were told all over the country of the new factory place, and the high wages that were offered to all classes of work people; stories that reached the ears of mechanics' and farmers' sons and gave new life to lonely and dependent women in distant towns and farm houses. . . . Troops of young girls came from different parts of New England, and from Canada, and men were employed to collect them at so much a head, and deliver them at the factories.

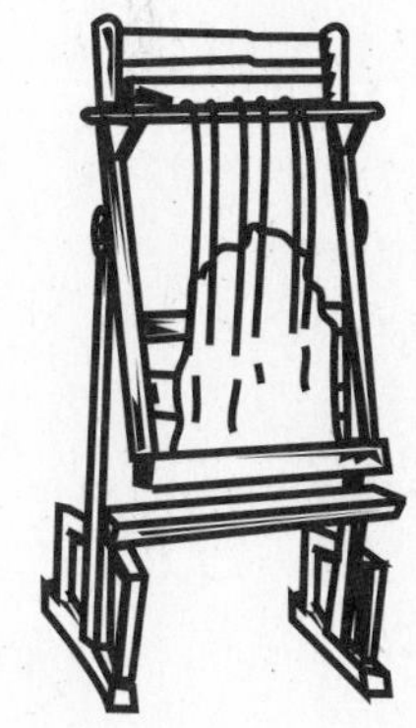

At the time the Lowell cotton mills were started the caste of the factory girl was the lowest among the employments of women. In England and in France, particularly, great injustice had been done to her real character. She was represented as subjected to influences that must destroy her purity and self-respect. In the eyes of her overseer she was but a brute, a slave, to be beaten, pinched and pushed about. It was to overcome this prejudice that such high wages had been offered to women that they might be induced to become mill girls, in spite of the opprobrium that still clung to this degrading occupation. . . .

The early mill girls were of different ages. Some were not over ten years old; a few were in middle life, but the majority were between the ages of sixteen and twenty-five. The very young girls were called "doffers." They "doffed," or took off, the full bobbins from the spinning frames, and replaced them with empty ones. These mites worked about fifteen minutes every hour and the rest of

vocations: occupations
incumbrance: burden

the time was their own. When the overseer was kind they were allowed to read, knit, or go outside the mill yard to play. They were paid two dollars a week. The working hours of all the girls extended from five o'clock in the morning until seven in the evening, with one half hour each, for breakfast and dinner. Even the doffers were forced to be on duty nearly fourteen hours a day. This was the greatest hardship in the lives of these children. Several years later a ten-hour law was passed, but not until long after some of these little doffers were old enough to appear before the legislative committee on the subject, and plead, by their presence, for a reduction of the hours of labor.

Those of the mill girls who had homes generally worked from eight to ten months in the year; the rest of the time was spent with parents or friends. A few taught school during the summer months. Their life in the factory was made pleasant to them. In those days there was no need of advocating the doctrine of the proper relation between employer and employed. *Help was too valuable to be ill-treated.* . . .

The most prevailing incentive to labor was to secure the means of education for some *male* member of the family. To make a *gentleman* of a brother or a son, to give him a college education, was the dominant thought in the minds of a great many of the better class of mill girls. I have known more than one to give every cent of her wages, month after month, to her brother, that he might get the education necessary to enter some profession. I have known a mother to work years in this way for her boy. I have known women to educate young men by their earnings, who were not sons or relatives. There are many men now living who were helped to an education by the wages of the early mill girls.

It is well to digress here a little, and speak of the influence the possession of money had on the characters of some of these women. We can hardly realize what a change the cotton factory made in the status of the working women. Hitherto woman had always been a money *saving* rather than a money earning, member of the community. Her labor could command but small return. If she worked out as servant, or "help," her wages were from 50 cents to $1.00 a week; or, if she went from house to house by the day to spin and weave, or do tailoress work, she could get but 75 cents a week and her meals. As teacher, her services were not in demand, and the arts, the professions, and even the trades and industries, were nearly all closed to her.

As late as 1840 there were only seven vocations outside the home into which the women of New England had entered. At this time woman had no property rights. A widow could be left without her share of her husband's (or the family) property, an "incumbrance" to his estate. A father could make his will without reference to his daughter's share of the inheritance. He usually left her a home on the farm as long as she remained single. A woman was not supposed to be capable of spending her own, or of using other people's money. In Massachusetts, before 1840, a woman could not, legally, be treasurer of her own sewing society, unless some man were responsible for her. The law took no cognizance of woman as a money spender. She was a ward, an appendage, a relict. Thus it happened that if a woman did not choose to marry, or, when left a widow, to remarry, she had no choice but to enter one of the few employments open to her, or to become a burden on the charity of some relative.

cognizance: recognition

relict: solitary, left-over being

incendiary: willfully stirring up rebellion

One of the first strikes that ever took place in this country was in Lowell in 1836. When it was announced that the wages were to be cut down, great indignation was felt, and it was decided to strike or "turn out" en masse. This was done. The mills were shut down, and the girls went from their several corporations in procession to the grove on Chapel Hill, and listened to incendiary speeches from some early labor reformers.

One of the girls stood on a pump and gave vent to the feelings of her companions in a neat speech, declaring that it was their duty to resist all attempts at cutting down the wages. This was the first time a woman had spoken in public in Lowell, and the event caused surprise and consternation among her audience.

It is hardly necessary to say that, so far as practical results are concerned, this strike did no good. The corporation would not come to terms. The girls were soon tired of holding out, and they went back to their work at the reduced rate of wages. The ill success of this early attempt at resistance on the part of the wage element seems to have made a precedent for the issue of many succeeding strikes.

Discussion Questions

1. **Why do you think Harriet Robinson wanted to write about the mill girls?**
2. **Why did girls come from all over the country to work in the Lowell mills?**
3. **How might the lives of women have changed when they began to earn money in the cotton factories?**

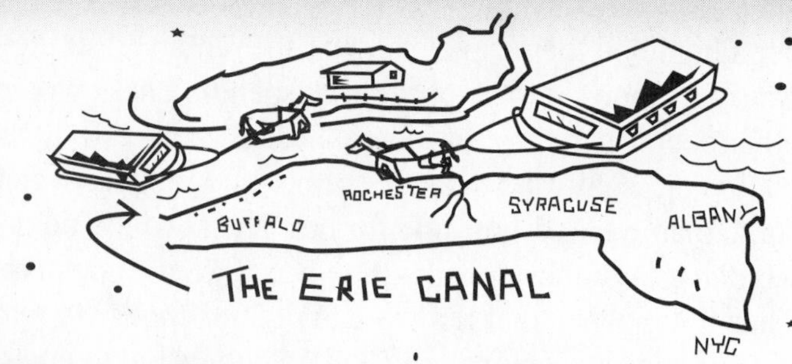

The Erie Canal

This famous folk song is about a bargeman on the Erie Canal and his mule, Sal. If possible, play a tape or CD of the song.

lock: dammed-off section of a canal where the boat is raised or lowered to a new water level

I've got a mule, her name is Sal,
Fifteen years on the Erie Canal.
She's a good ol' worker and a good ol' pal,
Fifteen years on the Erie Canal.
We've hauled some barges in our day,
Filled with lumber, coal, and hay,
And we know ev'ry inch of the way,
From Albany to Buffalo.

Chorus:
Low bridge, ev'rybody down!
Low bridge, for we're comin' to a town!
And you'll always know your neighbor,
You'll always know your pal,
If you've ever navigated on the Erie Canal.

We better get on our way, old pal,
Fifteen years on the Erie Canal.
'Cause you bet your life I'd never part with Sal,
Fifteen years on the Erie Canal.
Get up there mule, here comes a lock,
We'll make Rome 'bout six o'clock,
One more trip and back we'll go,
Right back home to Buffalo.

Discussion Questions

1. **What can you tell about the bargeman's job from the song?**
2. **Why do you think this song has continued to be sung?**

Encourage students to gather information about the kinds of people and goods carried on the Erie Canal between the Great Lakes and New York City in the early 1800s.

from

Declaration of Sentiments and Resolutions

These excerpts are taken from Elizabeth Cady Stanton's 1848 Declaration of Sentiments and from the Resolutions created at the women's rights convention in Seneca Falls, New York, that year.

Now, in view of this entire disfranchisement of one-half the people of this country, their social and religious degradation, in view of the unjust laws above mentioned, and because women do feel themselves aggrieved, oppressed, and fraudulently deprived of their most sacred rights, we insist that they have immediate admission to all the rights and privileges which belong to them as citizens of the United States.

In entering upon the great work before us, we anticipate no small amount of misconception, misrepresentation, and ridicule; but we shall use every instrumentality within our power to effect our object. We shall employ agents, circulate tracts, petition the state and national legislatures, and endeavor to enlist the pulpit and the press in our behalf. We hope this Convention will be followed by a series of conventions embracing every part of the country.

disfranchisement: state of being deprived of the rights of citizenship
instrumentality: means
tracts: persuasive pamphlets
precept: law
coeval: living in the same era
mediately: through an agency
race: the human race

Resolutions

Whereas, the great precept of nature is conceded to be that "man shall pursue his own true and substantial happiness." Blackstone in his *Commentaries* remarks that this law of nature, being coeval with mankind and dictated by God himself, is, of course, superior in obligation to any other. It is binding over all the globe, in all countries and at all times; no human laws are of any validity if contrary to this, and such of them as are valid derive all their force, and all their validity, and all their authority, mediately and immediately, from this original; therefore, . . .

Resolved, that all laws which prevent woman from occupying such a station in society as her conscience shall dictate, or which place her in a position inferior to that of man, are contrary to the great precept of nature and therefore of no force or authority.

Resolved, that woman is man's equal, was intended to be so by the Creator, and the highest good of the race demands that she should be recognized as such.

Resolved, that the women of this country ought to be enlightened in regard to the laws under which they live, that they may no longer publish their degradation by declaring themselves satisfied with their present position, nor their ignorance, by asserting that they have all the rights they want. . . .
Resolved, that it is the duty of the women of this country to secure to themselves their sacred right to the elective franchise. . . .
Resolved, therefore, that, being invested by the Creator with the same capabilities and same consciousness of responsibility for their exercise, it is demonstrably the right and duty of woman, equally with man, to promote every righteous cause by every righteous means.

Discussion Questions

1. **Do you agree that it is a basic law of nature that "man shall pursue his own true and substantial happiness"? Why or why not?**
2. **How would life be different today if women were not considered citizens?**

from

On the Chesapeake

by Frederick Douglass

This essay vividly conveys the pain of slavery.

Our house stood within a few rods of the Chesapeake Bay, whose broad bosom was ever white with sail from every quarter of the habitable globe. Those beautiful vessels robed in purest white, so delightful to the eye of freemen were to me so many shrouded ghosts, to terrify and torment me with thoughts of my wretched condition.

I have often . . . stood all alone upon the lofty banks of that noble bay, and traced . . . the countless number of sails moving off to the mighty ocean. The sight of these always affected me powerfully. My thoughts would compel utterance; and there, with no audience but the Almighty, I would pour out my soul's complaint . . . with an apostrophe to the moving multitude of ships:

"You are loosed from your moorings and are free; I am fast in my chains, and am a slave! You move merrily before the gentle gale, and I sadly before the bloody whip! You are freedom's swift-winged angels, that fly round the world; I am confined in bands of iron! O that I were free! O, that I were on one of your gallant decks, and under your protecting wing! Alas! In betwixt me and you, the turbid waters roll. Go on, go on. O that I could also go! Could I but swim! If I could fly! O, why was I born a man, of whom to make a brute!

"The glad ship is gone; she hides in the dim distance. I am left in the hottest hell of unending slavery. O god, save me! God deliver me! Let me be free! Is there any God? Why am I a slave? I will run away. I will not stand it. . . . Only think of it; one hundred miles straight north, and I am free! Try it? Yes! God help me, I will. It cannot be that I shall live and die a slave. I will take to the water. This very bay shall yet bear me into freedom."

rods: units of measure, each about 16 1/2 feet

apostrophe: an address to a thing or an absent person

moorings: fastenings to hold a boat or ship

Discussion Questions

1. **If you could choose a metaphor for your freedom, as Douglass chose the sailboats for his, what would it be?**
2. **Why might Douglass wish that he were not born a man?**

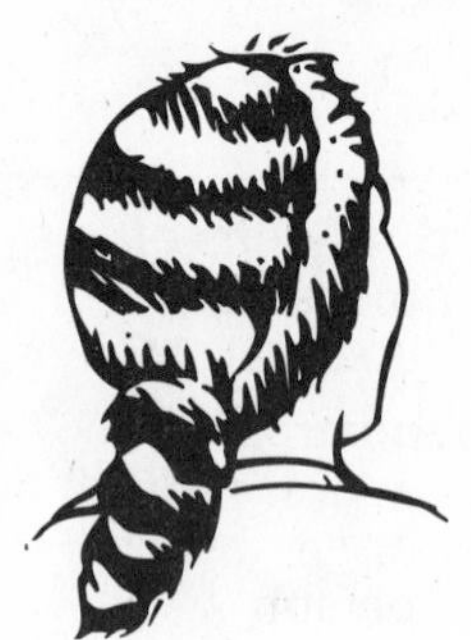

from

Davy Crockett: Defender of the Alamo

by William R. Sanford and Carl R. Green

In the excerpt below, these biographers of David "Davy" Crockett recount some of the legendary woodsman's travels and tall tales, his proud departure from Tennessee after losing an election, and his final sacrifice for Texas at the Alamo.

exploits: adventures

America loved Davy's tall tales—and half-believed them. If Davy said he could "grin" a raccoon out of a tree, few would doubt him. In 1834, with Thomas Chilton's help, Davy wrote his life story. The book retold Davy's adventures and blasted his foes. *Narrative of the Life of Davy Crockett of the State of Tennessee, Written by Himself,* became a best-seller.

In the spring of 1834, Davy toured the major cities of the East. At Bunker Hill, he said he felt he was standing on holy ground. In Philadelphia his fans gave him a fine new rifle. Davy named the gun Pretty Betsy. He described the trip in *An Account of Col. Crockett's Tour to the North and Down East.* That book, too, was a best-seller.

The almanacs of the day printed weather and crop information. As Davy's fame grew, the almanacs increased sales by adding tall tales of his exploits. Did Davy cross the Mississippi on stilts? Did he fight the Battle of New Orleans from the back of an alligator? The Crockett almanacs swore he did.

Wooden-legged Adam Huntsman challenged Davy in the election of 1835. "Timber Toes" raked up all the old tales of Davy's [misbehavior]. Davy mostly ignored the charges. He toured the district, telling stories and basking in the warmth of the crowds. To his surprise, the old tactics did not work. Davy lost his seat by 252 votes. The Jackson camp, he protested, had paid $25 a head for Huntsman's winning votes.

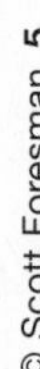

During the campaign, Davy had made a promise. If elected, he said he would give the voters his best. If not, the voters "might all go to h___ , and I would go to Texas." Davy was drawn by the lure of cheap land. Here was a chance to pay off debts and make a new start.

fandango: lively Spanish dance

Davy was as good as his word. He grabbed Old Betsy and set out for Texas. By the time he reached the Texas border, he was low on cash. He solved the problem by swapping his watch for a cheaper one and $30. By then his party had grown to sixteen or more "Crockett men." All had heard the same rumors. Texas would soon fight for its freedom from Mexico.

At each stop, Davy was hailed as a hero. In Nacogdoches, he and his friends took an oath of loyalty to Texas. On February 6, 1836, the party reached San Antonio. At the Alamo, the garrison threw a *fandango* in Davy's honor. The dance was in full swing when a messenger rode in with a warning. The Mexican army was advancing toward San Antonio.

General Santa Anna laid siege to the Alamo on February 23. The Texans held his forces at bay for thirteen long, bloody days. Davy was everywhere, urging the men to do their duty. The final assault breached the walls on March 6. The defenders died to the last man.

Davy Crockett died a hero's death that day in 1836. Since then, his story has been told and retold in books, plays, and films.

Discussion Questions

1. **Why do you think people told tall tales about Davy Crockett?**
2. **Do you think Davy Crockett made a better politician or soldier? Explain.**

from

Levi Strauss: Blue Jean Tycoon

by Meish Goldish

In this excerpt from a biography of Levi Strauss, we learn how a good businessman with drive and imagination could be successful on the frontier, especially during the California Gold Rush.

Because of the gold rush, San Francisco was growing at an astounding rate. In 1850, the year California became a state, San Francisco had about 25,000 people in it. Three years later, its population reached almost 70,000. . . .

Outside the city, fortune seekers worked and lived in "diggings." Finding gold was difficult, and it took its toll on both the miners and their clothing.

Before Levi Strauss even stepped off his ship, he discovered how well a peddler in California might do. Nearly his entire stock of goods was bought right on board! All he had left were a few bolts (large pieces) of canvas. Levi had brought the tough cloth to sell to miners for tents and wagon covers.

At the wharf, Levi was met by his sister Fanny and his brother-in-law David. The couple was delighted to have Levi move in with them. They offered him work at David's dry-goods store in San Francisco.

In the store, David and Levi sold cloth, canvas, blankets, cups, dishes, and other items. They also sold shirts and pants. Most of the merchandise arrived by ship from New York. Levi's brothers, Jonas and Louis, supplied large bolts of canvas and other fabric to the California store. . . .

In 1856, the two men moved into an even larger store. They sold both retail and wholesale. (Retail means selling small amounts of goods to individual customers. Wholesale means selling large amounts of goods to owners of other stores.)

Levi Strauss & Co.

Soon Levi and David were equal partners in the business, along with Jonas and Louis in New York. However, they could not call their company "Strauss Brothers." That name had already been taken by another firm in San Francisco. The family agreed that Levi had the best mind for business, so they called themselves "Levi Strauss & Co."

Sales were brisk in the new San Francisco store, but Levi wanted to grow even bigger. Living up to his reputation, he soon found another way to increase business. He knew that many miners outside the city could not easily get back to San Francisco for fresh supplies, so Levi himself went out to the diggings. Using a horse and wagon, he peddled his wares from camp to camp. . . .

Jeans: An Accidental Discovery

No one knows for sure exactly when Levi got the idea for his now-famous "Levi's jeans," but a popular legend goes like this: One day in the diggings, Levi met a miner and offered to sell him canvas for a tent. The miner didn't need a tent, but he asked if Levi had any rugged overalls to sell him. He explained that his clothing didn't last very long, since he spent many hours on his knees panning near streams.

Suddenly, Levi had a brainstorm! He told the miner he would deliver his overalls in a few days. Then he went off to find a tailor to cut his canvas fabric into a pair of work pants. The miner was very pleased with this rugged new clothing. Soon other miners were asking for the same canvas pants. Levi had accidentally discovered his own special gold mine.

Levi rushed off a letter to Jonas and Louis, asking them to ship more canvas. Since they were out of canvas at the time, denim was sent instead. Denim, a heavy cotton material, came from the French town of Nimes. . . .

Word about Levi's new denim pants spread rapidly throughout California. Travelers soon brought news of the pants to other parts of the West and Southwest. Cowboys were interested in the denim pants because they were tough enough to last during long rides in the saddle. Railroad workers and farmers who lived west of the Mississippi were also among the first to ask for a pair of "Levi's."

Levi and David could hardly keep up with the demand for their new creation. Their business was growing by leaps and bounds, but it wasn't from jeans alone. Miners began bringing their families to San Francisco to settle, so Levi Strauss & Co. was soon selling dresses and children's clothing. Levi himself gained a reputation in and around California as a dependable and honest businessperson.

Discussion Questions

1. **In your opinion, why was Levi Strauss so successful?**
2. **What do you think would be the difficulties of being a merchant during Gold Rush times in California?**

from

Lincoln's Inaugural Address

In these excerpts from his inaugural address, given on March 4, 1861, President Abraham Lincoln tries to assure the South that he supports states' rights, saying that he will uphold the Fugitive Slave Law and will not send federal troops without provocation.

accession: attainment of power
recanted: withdrew beliefs formerly held
institutions: established laws, customs, practices

Fellow citizens of the United States: in compliance with a custom as old as the government itself, I appear before you to address you briefly and to take, in your presence, the oath prescribed by the Constitution of the United States, to be taken by the President "before he enters on the execution of his office. . . ."

[States rights]

Apprehension seems to exist among the people of the Southern States that by the accession of a Republican administration their property and their peace and personal security are to be endangered. There has never been any reasonable cause for such apprehension. Indeed, the most ample evidence to the contrary has all the while existed and been open to their inspection. It is found in nearly all the published speeches of him who now addresses you. I do but quote from one of those speeches when I declare that "I have no purpose, directly or indirectly, to interfere with the institution of slavery where it exists. I believe I have no lawful right to do so, and I have no inclination to do so." Those who nominated and elected me did so with full knowledge that I had made this and many similar declarations, and had never recanted them. And, more than this, they placed in the platform for my acceptance, and as a law to themselves and to me, the clear and emphatic resolution which I now read:

"Resolved: that the maintenance inviolate of the rights of the States, and especially the right of each State to order and control its own domestic institutions according to its own judgment exclusively, is essential to that balance of power on which the perfection and endurance of our political fabric depend, and we denounce the lawless invasion by armed force of the soil of any State or Territory, no matter under what pretext, as among the gravest of crimes." . . .

[Fugitive Slave Law]

There is much controversy about the delivering up of fugitives from service or labor. The clause I now read is as plainly written in the Constitution as any other of its provisions:

"No person held to service or labor in one State, under the laws thereof, escaping into another, shall in consequence of any law or regulation therein be discharged from such service or labor, but shall be delivered up on claim of the party to whom such service or labor may be due."

It is scarcely questioned that this provision was intended by those who made it for the reclaiming of what we call fugitive slaves; and the intention of the lawgiver is the law. . . .

provision: legal statement requiring something specific

perpetuity: endlessness

duties and imposts: taxes

[The Union]

In 1787 one of the declared objects for ordaining and establishing the Constitution was "to form a more perfect union."

But if the destruction of the Union by one or by a part only of the States be lawfully possible, the Union is less perfect than before the Constitution, having lost the vital element of perpetuity.

It follows from these views that no State upon its own mere motion can lawfully get out of the Union; that Resolves and Ordinances to that effect are legally void; and that acts of violence, within any State or States, against the authority of the United States, are insurrectionary or revolutionary, according to circumstances.

I therefore consider that, in view of the Constitution and the laws, the Union is unbroken; and to the extent of my ability I shall take care, as the Constitution itself expressly enjoins upon me, that the laws of the Union be faithfully executed in all the States. Doing this I deem to be only a simple duty on my part; and I shall perform it so far as practicable, unless my rightful masters, the American people, shall withhold the requisite means, or in some authoritative manner direct the contrary. I trust this will not be regarded as a menace, but only as the declared purpose of the Union that it will Constitutionally defend and maintain itself.

In doing this there needs to be no bloodshed or violence; and there shall be none, unless it be forced upon the national authority. The power confided to me will be used to hold, occupy, and possess the property and places belonging to the government, and to collect the duties and imposts; but beyond what may be necessary for these objects, there will be no invasion, no using of force against or among the people anywhere. . . .

That there are persons in one section or another who seek to destroy the Union at all events, and are glad of any pretext to do it, I will neither affirm nor deny; but if there be such, I need address no word to them. To those, however, who really love the Union may I not speak?

Before entering upon so grave a matter as the destruction of our national fabric, with all its benefits, its memories, and its hopes, would it not be wise to ascertain precisely why we do it? Will you hazard so desperate a step while there is any possibility that any portion of the ills you fly from have no real existence? Will you, while the certain ills you fly to are greater than all the real ones you fly from—will you risk the commission of so fearful a mistake?

All profess to be content in the Union if all Constitutional rights can be maintained. Is it true, then, that any right, plainly written in the Constitution, has been denied? I think not. . . .

[Possibility of Civil War]

In your hands, my dissatisfied fellow-countrymen, and not in mine, is the momentous issue of civil war. The government will not assail you. You can have no conflict without being yourselves the aggressors. You have no oath registered in heaven to destroy the government, while I shall have the most solemn one to "preserve, protect, and defend it."

I am loathe to close. We are not enemies, but friends. We must not be enemies. Though passion may have strained, it must not break our bonds of affection. The mystic chords of memory, stretching from every battlefield and patriot grave to every living heart and hearthstone all over this broad land, will yet swell the chorus of the Union when again touched, as surely they will be, by the better angels of our nature.

Discussion Questions

1. **Why do you think Lincoln felt so strongly about maintaining the Union?**
2. **What does Lincoln say to calm the fears of the southern citizens?**
3. **If you had lived during Lincoln's time, would you have supported his stand on states' rights? Why or why not?**

from

Steal Away

by Jennifer Armstrong

Bethlehem, the enslaved African American girl in *Steal Away,* secretly learns to read with the help of Susannah, a white girl from Vermont. In this excerpt, the two are about to run away from the Virginia farm owned by Susannah's uncle. The excerpt begins from Susannah's point of view. She speaks to Bethlehem.

"Beth, I have to leave tomorrow. Tomorrow."

I leaned my head back and stared at the stars. They could not be the same stars that wheeled above New England. How could they be? How could this be the same world? Bats careened above me, jagged particles of night. My mind was a blank.

careened: lurched from side to side

"I'm going with you."

I was still staring at the stars, the bats like winks across my vision. Slowly, I heard in my head what Bethlehem had just spoken out loud. "What?"

Bethlehem drew a shuddering breath. I realized she was crying, or trying not to. "I can help you if you help me."

"But—"

"They'll think we got stolen by those slave-stealing men," she whispered. "I saw it in a news sheet." . . .

"Beth. You can't." We stared at each other. All I could see of her were her eyes. She looked down at the ground.

What if she were to betray me? I wondered then. Once alert my uncle, and I would never have another chance. I considered carefully. To my way of thinking, I had already begun my journey and must not halt or falter.

"Very well. We'll go tomorrow."

She raised her eyes finally and looked at me. Then she nodded once and turned away.

Bethlehem: I swear, my knees were so weak I could hardly hold myself up. . . . Any minute, they would storm in and take me away, sell me south or worse. I would never have another chance to let such craziness pass my lips.

notion: idea

But nobody came. The dogs did not bark; no lights shone anywhere. . . . Tonight I would find clothes for myself, and tomorrow I would leave with Susannah.

With Susannah.

Again I found myself trembling, but I clutched the bundle and hurried outside for a breath of air. Above me, the stars spread out in their multitudes. . . .

A breeze came up and parted the branches to my left. There I saw the dipper, the gourd in the sky pointing to the North Star. I had no notion how far away Vermont was, but it was North and that was where I needed to go. I was going to get there with a knife, some matches, and a white girl dressed as a boy.

Susannah: I awoke early the next morning, filled with hope. The prospect of leaving that hated place overcame the apprehensiveness I felt about taking Bethlehem along with me. I took my small shears from my sewing box, rolled them in a handkerchief, and put them in my pocket. It was one thing I could do to feel I was forwarding my plan. Then I sat by the window to watch the sun come up.

In the three months I had been in Virginia, I had started each day in this manner. I don't know why the first stirrings on the farm always made me so lonesome, but they did. . . . When Bethlehem walked out her door, I stood up, prickly with anticipation.

My scheme was still misty and shapeless. But all there was to do was get up and leave. Bethlehem and I would saddle the pony I always rode, and we would simply go. At some remote spot, I would transform myself into a boy. Beyond that, I knew only to strike north until we hit Vermont. What else was there to know? My lonesome feeling ebbed as the dawn spread across the horizon to the east and north, lighting my way.

"Morning, Miz Susannah," Bethlehem whispered to me as she entered my room.

I was smiling, but trying not to. I wanted her to know I was conscious of the gravity of our plan. Then I spoiled the effect by letting out a gasp.

"We're going!" I laughed breathlessly. I whirled around with my arms wide.

Discussion Questions

1. **Why do you think Susannah changed her mind about taking Bethlehem with her?**
2. **Why is Bethlehem more frightened than Susannah?**
3. **What dangers might lie ahead for the two girls?**

from

Uncle Tom's Cabin

by Harriet Beecher Stowe

In this excerpt, Eliza saves her small son from the slave trader in a superhuman feat of courage and physical strength.

vaulted: leaped
turbid: muddy

A thousand lives seemed to be concentrated in that one moment to Eliza. Her room opened by a side door to the river. She caught her child, and sprang down the steps towards it. The trader caught a full glimpse of her, just as she was disappearing down the bank; and throwing himself from his horse, and calling loudly on Sam and Andy, he was after her like a hound after a deer. In that dizzy moment her feet to her scarce seemed to touch the ground, and a moment brought her to the water's edge. Right on behind they came; and, nerved with strength such as God gives only to the desperate, with one wild cry and flying leap, she vaulted sheer over the turbid current by the shore, on to the raft of ice beyond. It was a desperate leap—impossible to anything but madness and despair; and Haley, Sam, and Andy, instinctively cried out, and lifted up their hands, as she did it.

The huge green fragment of ice on which she alighted pitched and creaked as her weight came on it, but she staid there not a moment. With wild cries and desperate energy she leaped to another and still another cake;—stumbling—leaping—slipping—springing upwards again! Her shoes are gone—her stockings cut from her feet—while blood marked every step; but she saw nothing, felt nothing, till dimly, as in a dream, she saw the Ohio side, and a man helping her up the bank.

"Yer a brave gal, now, whoever ye ar!" said the man, with an oath.

Eliza recognized the voice and face of a man who owned a farm not far from her old home.

arnt: earned

"O, Mr. Symmes!—save me—do save me—do hide me!" said Eliza.

"Why, what's this?' said the man. "Why, if 'tan't Shelby's gal!"

"My child!—this boy!—he'd sold him! There is his Mas'r," said she, pointing to the Kentucky shore. "O, Mr. Symmes, you've got a little boy!"

"So I have," said the man, as he roughly, but kindly, drew her up the steep bank. "Besides, you're a right brave gal. I like grit, wherever I see it."

When they had gained the top of the bank, the man paused.

"I'd be glad to do something for ye," said he; "but then there's nowhar I could take ye. The best I can do is to tell ye to go *thar*," said he, pointing to a large white house which stood by itself, off the main street of the village. "Go thar; they're kind folks. Thar's no kind o' danger but they'll help you, they're up to all that sort o' thing."

"The Lord bless you!" said Eliza, earnestly.

"No 'casion, no 'casion in the world," said the man. "What I've done's of no 'count."

"And, oh, surely, sir, you won't tell any one!"

"Go to thunder, gal! What do you take a feller for? In course not," said the man. "Come, now, go along like a likely, sensible gal, as you are. You've arnt your liberty, and you shall have it, for all me."

The woman folded her child to her bosom, and walked firmly and swiftly away. The man stood and looked after her.

"Shelby, now, mebbe won't think this yer the most neighborly thing in the world; but what's a feller to do? If he catches one of my gals in the same fix, he's welcome to pay back. Somehow I never could see no kind o' critter a strivin' and pantin', and trying to clar theirselves, with the dogs arter 'em, and go agin 'em. Besides, I don't see no kind of 'casion for me to be hunter and catcher for other folks, neither." . . .

Eliza made her desperate retreat across the river just in the dusk of twilight. The gray mist of evening, rising slowly from the river, enveloped her as she disappeared up the bank, and the swollen current and floundering masses of ice presented a hopeless barrier between her and her pursuer. Haley therefore slowly and discontentedly returned to the little tavern, to ponder further what was to be done.

Discussion Questions

1. **What are the narrator's feelings about Eliza?**
2. **Why do you think Mr. Symmes, a white man, helps Eliza and her son?**

from

The War Commenced

This article from the *New York Times* of April 13, 1861, about the first Civil War battle at Fort Sumter, includes messages sent among the Confederate Secretary of War L. P. Walker, his military commander General Pierre Beauregard, and Major Robert Anderson, the Union commander at Fort Sumter, that preceded the fall of the Union fort.

batteries: sets of heavy guns

breach: opening

Our Charleston Dispatches

Charleston, Friday, April 12.

The ball has opened. War is inaugurated.

The batteries of Sullivan's Island, Morris Island, and other points, were opened on Fort Sumpter at 4 o'clock this morning.

Fort Sumpter has returned the fire, and a brisk cannonading has been kept up. . . .

Charleston, Friday, April 12.

The firing has continued all day without intermission.

Two of Fort Sumpter's guns have been silenced, and it is reported that a breach has been made in the southeast wall.

The answer to Gen. Beauregard's demand by Major Anderson was that he would surrender when his supplies were exhausted, that is, if he was not reinforced.

Not a casualty has yet happened to any of the forces. . . .

Later Dispatches—Hostilities Still Proceeding. . . .

Charleston, Friday, April 12—3 A.M.

It is utterly impossible to reinforce Fort Sumpter, to-night, as a storm is now raging.

The mortar batteries will be playing on Fort Sumpter all night. . . .

Important Correspondence Preceding the Bombardment.

Charleston, Friday, April 12.

The following is the telegraphic correspondence between the War Department at Montgomery and Gen. Beauregard immediately preceding the hostilities. . . .

[No. 8.]

Charleston, April 11.

To L. P. Walker, Secretary of War:

Maj. Anderson replies:

"I have the honor to acknowledge the receipt of your

evacuation: giving up of military occupation

effusion: pouring forth

communication demanding the evacuation of this fort, and to say in reply thereto, that it is a demand with which I regret that my sense of honor and my obligations to my government will prevent my compliance."He adds: "Probably I will await the first shot, and if you do not batter us to pieces, we will be starved out in a few days."

Answer. G. F. Beauregard.

[No. 9]
Montgomery, April 11.
Gen. Beauregard—Charleston:

We do not desire needlessly to bombard Fort Sumpter, if Major Anderson will state the time at which, as indicated by him, he will evacuate, and agree that, in the meantime, he will not use his guns against us unless ours should be employed against Fort Sumpter. You are thus to avoid the effusion of blood. If this or its equivalent be refused, reduce the fort as your judgment decides to be the most practicable.

(Signed) L. P. Walker, Secretary of War.

The News in Washington.
Washington, Friday, April 12.

Everyone had been waiting anxiously all day for the report of an attack upon the Government supply vessels, which it was ascertained last evening would probably approach Charleston harbor some time during the night or this morning. The surprise occasioned by the report from repeated dispatches that they had entered the harbor without molestation, and were landing the supplies without any difficulty, present or apprehensive, created nearly as great an excitement as the later reports of battle. . . .

Cabinet Councils.

Mr. Lincoln summoned the cabinet. . . . There was general rejoicing at the prospects of peace and final adjustment of our national difficulties, dampened somewhat, however, by fear that it would prove false. . . . The War Department did not place any reliance to-day on the peace dispatches. Secretary Cameron declared that he saw no escape from conflict at both Forts Sumpter and Pickens.

Discussion Questions

1. **Why do you think the Southern troops did not attack the supply ships?**
2. **Do you think it is valuable to read original documents like these dispatches and messages? Explain why or why not.**

The Emancipation Proclamation

by Abraham Lincoln

The Emancipation Proclamation is given here in its entirety.

countervailing: opposing and equal in strength

Whereas, on the twenty-second day of September, in the year of our Lord one thousand eight hundred and sixty-two, a proclamation was issued by the President of the United States, containing, among other things, the following, to wit:

"That on the first day of January, in the year of our Lord one thousand eight hundred and sixty-three, all persons held as slaves within any State or designated part of a State, the people whereof shall then be in rebellion against the United States, shall be then, thenceforward, and forever free; and the Executive Government of the United States, including the military and naval authority thereof, will recognize and maintain the freedom of such persons, and will do no act or acts to repress such persons, or any of them, in any efforts they may make for their actual freedom.

"That the Executive will, on the first day of January aforesaid, by proclamation, designate the States and parts of States, if any, in which the people thereof, respectively, shall then be in rebellion against the United States; and the fact that any State, or the people thereof, shall on that day be, in good faith, represented in the Congress of the United States by members chosen thereto at elections wherein a majority of the qualified voters of such State shall have participated, shall, in the absence of strong countervailing testimony, be deemed conclusive evidence that such State, and the people thereof, are not then in rebellion against the United States."

Now, therefore I, Abraham Lincoln, President of the United States, by virtue of the power in me vested as Commander-in-Chief, of the Army and Navy of the United Sates in time of actual armed rebellion against the authority and government of the United States, and as a fit and necessary war measure for suppressing said rebellion, do, on this first day of January, in the year of our Lord one thousand eight hundred and sixty-three, and in accordance with my purpose so to do publicly proclaimed for the full period of one hundred days, from the day first above mentioned, order and designate as the States and parts of States wherein the people thereof respectively, are this day in rebellion against the United States, the following, to wit:

garrison: military post

invoke: call on for support

Arkansas, Texas, Louisiana, (except the Parishes of St. Bernard, Plaquemines, Jefferson, St. John, St. Charles, St. James Ascension, Assumption, Terrebonne, Lafourche, St. Mary, St. Martin, and Orleans, including the City of New Orleans) Mississippi, Alabama, Florida, Georgia, South Carolina, North Carolina, and Virginia, (except the forty-eight counties designated as West Virginia, and also the counties of Berkley, Accomac, Northampton, Elizabeth City, York, Princess Ann, and Norfolk, including the cities of Norfolk and Portsmouth[)] , and which excepted parts, are for the present, left precisely as if this proclamation were not issued.

And by virtue of the power, and for the purpose aforesaid, I do order and declare that all persons held as slaves within said designated States, and parts of States, are, and henceforward shall be free; and that the Executive government of the United States, including the military and naval authorities thereof, will recognize and maintain the freedom of said persons.

And I hereby enjoin upon the people so declared to be free to abstain from all violence, unless in necessary self-defence; and I recommend to them that, in all cases when allowed, they labor faithfully for reasonable wages.

And I further declare and make known, that such persons of suitable condition, will be received into the armed service of the United States to garrison forts, positions, stations, and other places, and to man vessels of all sorts in said service.

And upon this act, sincerely believed to be an act of justice, warranted by the Constitution, upon military necessity, I invoke the considerate judgment of mankind, and the gracious favor of Almighty God.

In witness whereof, I have hereunto set my hand and caused the seal of the United States to be affixed.

Done at the city of Washington, this first day of January, in the year of our Lord one thousand eight hundred and sixty three, and of the Independence of the United States of America the eighty-seventh.

By the President: Abraham Lincoln

William H. Seward, Secretary of State.

Discussion Questions

1. **Why do you think there were still enslaved people in the Confederate states after January 1, 1863?**
2. **Why might Lincoln have included the paragraph about receiving freed people into the U.S. armed service?**
3. **If you were the owner of a plantation in the South, how would you have reacted to the Emancipation Proclamation? If you were an enslaved person, how would you have felt about it?**

from

Angel of the Battlefield

by Ishbel Ross

This excerpt from a biography of Clara Barton shows her amazing stamina and compassion as a battlefield nurse.

scathing: harsh

As she watched the "shattered army streaming back into the capital" she picked out those "who looked the worst and limped the hardest" and drew them into her own quarters, to see what could be done for them. "All very new business," Clara commented.

But it was business she was learning fast—the true face of war. All through August and September she was in the city, visiting hospitals and wharves, and arranging her mounting supplies. She was constantly on the move, a small and vigorous figure meeting each emergency as it arose in the practical way that was to characterize all her later labors. She rounded up fellow lodgers, friends at the mess, and her New England relatives, to help her in her errands of mercy. The future of the Red Cross was already foreshadowed in the boxes, barrels, and bundles that Clara accumulated, dealing out supplies as fast as she could circulate.

She watched the army tighten up, the tension mount in the capital. Washington had come to life with a vengeance. Relief societies were in operation. Women circulated with delicacies for the soldiers. They attended the parades and flag raisings. They flirted and danced as well as sewed. Many now had cause to weep. Clara burned with indignation over army muddling and the lack of nurses. She was scathing over some of the belles who were enjoying the war. "I greatly fear that the few privileged, elegantly dressed ladies who ride over and sit in their carriages to witness 'splendid services' and 'inspect the Army of the Potomac' and come away 'delighted,' learn very little of what lies there under canvas," she wrote to the Ladies Relief Committee of Worcester on December 16, 1861. . . .

Back in Washington she put on a strong campaign to wear down the opposition she encountered at every turn. . . .

staunch: stop

With the persistence she later applied to founding the Red Cross in America, Clara went from one army official to another, pleading for passes, testing every possibility. She had her first success with Major D. H. Rucker, Assistant Quartermaster General in charge of transportation. She found him busy giving orders and permits at a desk behind a wicket fence with a gate in it.

"He was pressed, and anxious, and gruff, and I was very tired," Clara noted in her diary. She was so tired, in fact, that she burst into tears when he asked her what she wanted. He drew her inside his fence and told her to stop crying. He stared at her oddly when she said she wanted to get to the front. That was no place for a woman, he countered, pressing her for motive. Did she have a father or brother in the ranks?

Then Clara told him about her supplies. When he heard about her warehouse and her lodgings filled with good things from New England, he promptly gave her an order for wagons and the men to load them. "And here is your permit to go to the front," he added, "and God bless you."

Bit by bit Clara obtained all the necessary passes from the various Government departments. . . .

With her transportation assured at last, she went straight into action. "When our armies fought on Cedar Mountain, I broke the shackles and went to the field," she wrote. "And so began my work." Heading for Culpeper, she climbed over the wagon wheel and poised herself among her bales and bundles. Off rattled her mules, bearing Clara, a slight, vigorous woman of forty, without her hoop, wearing a plaid jacket, a dark skirt, and a kerchief. . . .

"I thought that night if heaven ever sent out a holy angel, she must be one, her assistance was so timely," said the grateful Dr. Dunn.

Clara gave fainting men bread. . . . She helped to staunch their wounds. After doing all she could on the field she returned to Culpeper, where she dealt out shirts to the wounded, made soup and applesauce, and produced bandages in quantity. . . . When a captain remarked to her, "Miss Barton, this is a rough and unseemly position for you, a woman, to occupy," Clara responded, "Is it not as rough and unseemly for these pain-racked men?"

Discussion Questions

1. **What aspects of Clara Barton's personality helped her achieve her aim of caring for soldiers on the battlefield?**
2. **Would you have wanted to work with Clara Barton in the Civil War? If so, what would you have liked to do? Explain your thoughts.**

from

Virginia's General: Robert E. Lee and the Civil War

by Albert Marrin

This excerpt from a biography of General Robert E. Lee gives a vivid account of Lee, Ulysses S. Grant, and the soldiers on both sides at the hour of surrender in Appomattox, Virginia. "Marse Robert" refers to General Lee. Philip H. Sheridan was a Union cavalry officer.

At daybreak, after a short bombardment, the Army of Northern Virginia charged for the last time. Exhausted as they were, the chance to hit back renewed the soldiers' energy. All went well, at first. Giving the Rebel yell, they took the Yankee positions, little more than shallow rifle pits, and pushed ahead, driving the discounted cavalrymen before them. But it could not last.

The cavalrymen suddenly parted and moved away from the center of the field. Behind them was a solid wall of blue. Sheridan's infantry, in a line of battle two miles wide, came forward. Off to their right, stood Sheridan with his mounted cavalry, ten thousand strong, backed by scores of big guns. They were silent and unmoving, their flags snapping in the breeze. With Sheridan in front and Meade pressing from behind, the Army of Northern Virginia was trapped. Its twenty-three thousand men faced eighty thousand enemy troops, with more arriving by the minute.

Lee was waiting a mile to the rear when a message came from Gordon, the assault leader. His men had been "fought to a frazzle," and he could make no headway.

So that was it. The dreaded moment had arrived. Marse Robert listened in silence, shook his head sadly, and declared: "Then there is nothing left me but to go and see General Grant, and I would rather die a thousand deaths." . . .

Lee waited under an apple tree while one officer rode out with a flag of truce and another carried a request to meet Grant. Around noon, word came that the Union commander would meet him in the village. The meeting place was a two-story brick house belonging to Wilmer McLean. . . .

Lee arrived first and waited in the parlor. Grant came half an hour later. What a contrast they made! The Confederate chief stood straight as a ramrod in his splendid uniform. Grant, slightly stoop-shouldered, a cigar stub clenched between his teeth, had hurried there straight from the field. He wore no sword, and his mud-spattered pants were tucked inside muddy boots. Only the three stars on his shoulder straps indicated his rank. But he radiated self-confidence, and was clearly the boss. . . .

Lee brought him to the point: He wanted to hear the surrender terms. President Lincoln had set out the basic principle a few days earlier: "Let 'em up easy. . . ."

Grant's terms were in line with the president's wishes. Lee and his men would be paroled on their promise not to fight again. Confederate officers could keep their pistols, swords, and horses; everything else must be surrendered at a formal ceremony. Lee accepted the terms, relieved that his men would not be marched off to prison camps. The only problem, he said, was that ordinary cavalrymen and gunners owned their own horses. Grant did not wait to be asked for a favor; he said they could take their animals home "to put in a crop." He also promised to see that the starving army was fed. Lee signed the surrender document and the meeting ended. . . .

The news spread like wildfire. The Yankees went wild. Victory! Victory! They had won the greatest war in American history. . . . "I cried and laughed by turns," recalled Colonel Elisha Hunt Rhodes, Second Rhode Island regiment. "I was never so happy in my life." Another compared it to all the Fourths of July, past and future, rolled into one. "The air is black with hats and boots, coats, knapsacks, shirts and cartridge boxes. They fall on each others' necks and laugh and cry by turns. Huge, lumbering, bearded men embrace and kiss like school-girls, then dance and sing and shout, stand on their heads and play leapfrog with each other."

The racket annoyed Grant. There was no need to gloat over their victory, he thought. . . . The war was over, and the Rebels were their countrymen again. No one could (or should) ask for more.

Discussion Questions

1. **How would you describe Grant's attitude toward the Rebels at the surrender? What effect do you think this might have on the aftermath of the war?**
2. **If you had been a Confederate soldier, how would you have felt when you heard of Lee's surrender?**

from

Our Great Loss

This *New York Times* front-page article, dated April 15, 1865, contains the official dispatch from the Secretary of War announcing Lincoln's death and an article describing the investigation of the crime.

Official Dispatches.

War Department, Washington, April 15—4:10 A.M.
To Major-Gen. Dix:

The President continues insensible and is sinking.

Secretary Seward remains without change.

Frederick Seward's skull is fractured in two places, besides a severe cut upon the head.

The attendant is still alive, but hopeless. Maj. Seward's wound is not dangerous.

It is now ascertained with reasonable certainty that two assassins were engaged in the horrible crime, Wilkes Booth being the one that shot the President, and the other, a companion of his, whose name is not known, but whose description is so clear that he can hardly escape. It appears from a letter found in Booth's trunk that the murder was planned before the 4th of March, but fell through then because the accomplice backed out until "Richmond could be heard from." Booth and his accomplice were at the livery stable at 6 o'clock last evening, and left there with their horses about 10 o'clock, or shortly before that hour.

It would seem that they had for several days been seeking their chance, but for some unknown reason it was not carried into effect until last night.

One of them has evidently made his way to Baltimore—the other has not yet been traced.

Edwin M. Stanton, Secretary of War.

War Department, Washington, April 15.
Major-Gen. Dix:

Abraham Lincoln died this morning at twenty-two minutes after seven o'clock.

Edwin M. Stanton, Secretary of War.

devolved: passed
procured: gotten
apprize: inform
accosted: approached and spoke to aggressively

War Department, Washington, April 15—3 P.M.
Maj. Gen. Dix, New York:

Official notice of the death of the late President Abraham Lincoln, was given by the heads of departments this morning to Andrew Johnson, Vice President, upon whom the constitution devolved the office of President. Mr. Johnson, upon receiving this notice, appeared before the Hon. Salmon P. Chase Chief-Justice of the United States, and took the oath of office, as President of the United States. . . .

The Assassination.
Further Details of the Murder—Narrow Escape of Secretary Stanton—Measures Taken to Prevent the Escape of the Assassins of the President.
Washington, Saturday, April 15.

The assassin of President Lincoln left behind him his hat and a spur.

The hat was picked up in the President's box, and has been identified by parties to whom it has been shown as the one belonging to the suspected man, and accurately described as the one belonging to the suspected man by other parties, not allowed to see it before describing it.

The spur was dropped upon the stage, and that also has been identified as the one procured at a stable where the same man hired a horse in the evening.

Two gentlemen, who went to the Secretary of War to apprize him of the attack on Mr. Lincoln, met at the residence of the former a man muffled in a cloak, who, when accosted by them, hastened away.

It had been Mr. Stanton's intention to accompany Mr. Lincoln to the theatre, and occupy the same box, but the press of business prevented.

It therefore seems evident that the aim of the plotters was to paralyze the country by at once striking down the head, the heart and the arm of the country.

As soon as the dreadful events were announced in the streets, Superintendent Richards, and his assistants, were at work to discover the assassin.

In a few moments the telegraph had aroused the whole police force of the city.

Discussion Questions

1. **Why do you think authorities believed there was a "plot to paralyze the country"?**
2. **Why do you think the *Times* published information about the assassination from many different sources?**

Honoring Chinese-American Laborers

by John T. Doolittle

U.S. Representative John T. Doolittle of California gave this speech to the House on April 29, 1999. He honored the Chinese-American laborers who built the Central Pacific Railroad in the 1860s.

payroll: list of employees
terrain: ground

Mr. Speaker, today I rise to honor the Chinese-American community and pay tribute to its ancestors' contribution to the building of the American transcontinental railroad.

On May 8th, the Colfax Area Historical Society in my Congressional District will place a monument along Highway 174 at Cape Horn, near Colfax, California to recognize the efforts of the Chinese in laying the tracks that linked the east and west coasts for the first time. With the California Gold Rush and the opening of the West came an increased interest in building a transcontinental railroad. To this end, the Central Pacific Railroad Company was established, and construction of the route East from Sacramento began in 1863. Although the beginning of the effort took place on relatively flat land, labor and financial problems were persistent, resulting in only 50 miles of track being laid in the first two years. Although the company needed over 5,000 workers, it only had 600 on the payroll by 1864.

Chinese labor was suggested, as they had already helped build the California Central Railroad, the railroad from Sacramento to Marysville and the San Jose Railway. Originally thought to be too small to complete such a momentous task, Charles Crocker of Central Pacific pointed out, "The Chinese made the Great Wall, didn't they?"

The first Chinese were hired in 1865 at approximately $28 per month to do the very dangerous work of blasting and laying ties over the treacherous terrain of the high Sierras. They lived in simple dwellings and cooked their own meals, often consisting of fish, dried oysters and fruit, mushrooms and seaweed.

Work in the beginning was slow and difficult. After the first 23 miles, Central Pacific faced the daunting task of laying tracks over terrain that rose 7,000 feet in 100 miles. To conquer the many sheer embankments, the Chinese workers used techniques they had learned in China to complete similar tasks. They were lowered by

interior: inland from the coast

ropes from the top of cliffs in baskets, and while suspended, they chipped away at the granite and planted explosives that were used to blast tunnels. Many workers risked their lives and perished in the harsh winters and dangerous conditions.

By the summer of 1868, 4,000 workers, two thirds of which were Chinese, had built the transcontinental railroad over the Sierras and into the interior plains. On May 10, 1869, the two railroads were to meet at Promontory, Utah in front of a cheering crowd and a band. A Chinese crew was chosen to lay the final ten miles of track, and it was completed in only twelve hours.

Without the efforts of the Chinese workers in the building of America's railroads, our development and progress as a nation would have been delayed by years. Their toil in severe weather, cruel working conditions and for meager wages cannot be under appreciated. My sentiments and thanks go out to the entire Chinese-American community for its ancestors' contribution to the building of this great Nation.

Discussion Questions

1. **Why do you think Congressman Doolittle gave this speech?**
2. **Why might the Chinese workers have left China for California?**
3. **Was it a good idea for the railroad to hire the Chinese workers? Why or why not?**

Students may want to find out more about Chinese workers in the West in the nineteenth century or about building the transcontinental railroad. Encourage them to research the topics online or in the library.

from

The Homestead Act

The 1862 Homestead Act tells how to get 160 acres of land in the Great Plains.

161. Entry of unappropriated public lands

Every person who is the head of a family, or who has arrived at the age of twenty-one years, and is a citizen of the United States, or who has filed his declaration of intention to become such, as required by the naturalization laws, shall be entitled to enter one-quarter section, or a less quantity, of unappropriated public lands . . . ; but no person who is the proprietor of more than one hundred and sixty acres of land in any State or Territory, shall acquire any right under the homestead law. And every person owning and residing on land may, under the provisions of this section, enter other land lying contiguous to his land, which shall not, with the land so already owned and occupied, exceed in the aggregate one hundred and sixty acres.

unappropriated: not taken for anyone's use

proprietor: owner

affidavit: written statement made on an oath

syndicate: association formed to carry out a financial project

speculation: buy or sell in the face of high risk

162. Application for entry; affidavit

Any person applying to enter land under section 161 of this title shall first make and subscribe before the proper officer and file in the proper land office an affidavit that he or she is the head of a family, or is over twenty-one years of age, and that such application is honestly and in good faith made for the purpose of actual settlement and cultivation . . . that he or she is not acting as agent of any person, corporation, or syndicate in making such entry . . . that he or she does not apply to enter the same for the purpose of speculation, but in good faith to obtain a home for himself, or herself . . . and upon filing such affidavit with the officer designated by the Secretary of the Interior on payment of $5 when the entry is of not more than eighty acres, and on payment of $10 when the entry is for more than eighty acres, he or she shall thereupon be permitted to enter the amount of land specified.

Discussion Questions

1. **Why does the Homestead Act state that people wanting to claim a homestead must actually live on it and cultivate it?**
2. **Why do you think the U.S. government wanted people to settle on the Great Plains?**

Charles Goodnight

by Geoffrey Ward

This excerpt from *The West: An Illustrated History* tells about trail boss Charles Goodnight. When he returned to Texas after the Civil War, Goodnight found the cattle population doubled, and many rustlers were stealing cattle. Goodnight slowly and honestly built his own herd and developed a plan for getting them to market.

panhandle: strip of land projecting like the handle of a pan

Goodnight prized honesty and hard work. "Only the weak steal," he once said, and the only way to make an honest profit in cattle was to try to take them north to better markets. He needed a partner and enlisted the help of Oliver Loving, twenty-five years older than he, who had taken Texas herds all the way to Chicago before the war, something no other cattleman had ever done. What Goodnight now proposed was a new, seven-hundred-mile route to new destinations—the Indian reservation at Bosque Redondo, the mining camps of Colorado, and finally the Union Pacific crews working their way across Wyoming. Loving agreed to try it: Goodnight's plan, which required that herds be driven across Comanche hunting grounds, was full of risk, but also possibility.

In 1866, with 2,000 cattle and eighteen cowboys, the two men set out along what would soon be called the Goodnight-Loving Trail. To avoid the Comanche of the panhandle, they first went southwest, across an arid eighty-mile plain toward the Pecos River —"the most desolate country," Goodnight remembered, "that I ever explored." It took three days and three nights in choking dust without stopping to cross. Newborn calves slowed down the herd. . . . (On subsequent drives he would bring along an extra wagon just to carry the calves—each one wrapped in a burlap bag, so that it kept its own scent and its mother could find it when the calves were turned loose to feed at night.) Three hundred cattle died in the heat; a hundred more drowned when the thirst-crazed herd finally smelled the Pecos River and stampeded over its banks into quicksand and swirling waters.

Goodnight and Loving pointed the survivors north, into New Mexico Territory, and at last reached Bosque Redondo, where some 8,000 Navajo were on the verge of starvation and government agents gladly paid top dollar for Texas beef to feed them. The partners now had a $12,000 profit and half the herd still in their possession. They drove them even farther north, into Colorado, fattening their animals on range grasses as they traveled, then sold them in Denver. There, Loving learned that good grazing extended all the way to Montana, where other Indian agencies and military outposts were paying high prices. Excited about their prospects and $24,000 richer, the partners returned to Texas, bought more cattle, and hurried back up the trail they'd blazed.

blazed: created

Discussion Questions

1. **What were some of the difficulties of a cattle drive?**
2. **What do you think Goodnight meant when he said "only the weak steal"?**
3. **Do you think the goals of Goodnight and Loving were different from those of the eighteen cowboys on the trail with them? Explain.**

Students may want to research cattle drives online or in the library and make a report to the class on some aspect that interests them.

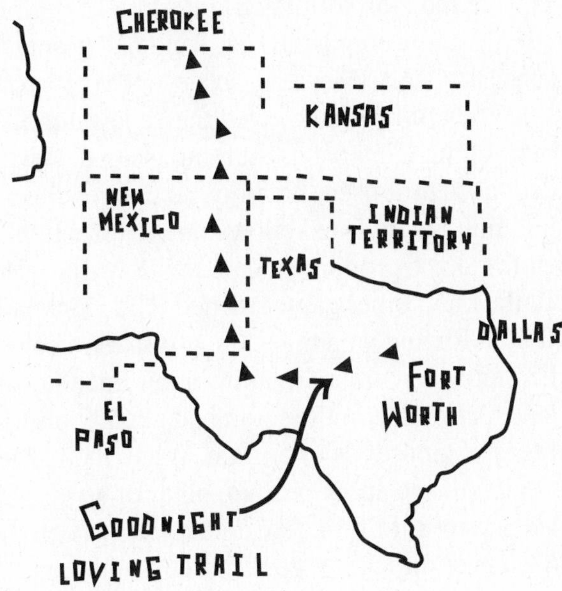

from

Sitting Bull: Sioux Leader

by Elizabeth Schleichert

This excerpt from a biography of Sitting Bull describes one of his gestures of peaceful but daring resistance against the Union Pacific Railroad as it cut through Lakota hunting grounds in the Yellowstone Valley.

surveyors: people who measure boundaries of tracts of land

unceded: not transferred legally

For Sitting Bull, things worsened in the early 1870s. At this time officials of the Northern Pacific Railroad determined that they wanted to build a line connecting St. Paul, Minnesota, with Seattle, Washington. They started sending surveyors to Sioux territory in the fall of 1871. The rail line intersected the Yellowstone Valley. This was the heart of the Hunkpapas' hunting ground. It was also part of the unceded lands promised the Sioux as their exclusive domain by the Fort Laramie Treaty. The Yellowstone River ran through a wide, lush valley filled with cottonwood and willow trees. Here, huge herds of buffalo and other game roamed. The Hunkpapas had recently fought for and won this valley from the Crows. There was no way the Sioux were going to allow a rail line to ruin their beloved land. A rail line to the south had already resulted in the killing of tens of thousands of buffalo. White men rode the railroads equipped with guns to shoot buffalo, both for sport and profit. Buffalo hides were sold for a few dollars each. Then they were shipped back East for leather goods, robes, and rugs. More than three million of these animals were slaughtered between 1872 and 1874. (By 1880 the herds were completely destroyed.) If the railroad came through Hunkpapa territory, it would mean the end of their buffalo, too. . . .

Plans for a Railroad

In August 1872, a second railroad surveying expedition arrived. It was accompanied by two groups of soldiers. Sitting Bull and his warriors were encamped not far away on the Powder River. They kept an eye on the surveyors, who were working along the south bank of the Yellowstone River under heavy cavalry escort. A railroad was being planned here. This was a violation of the Fort Laramie Treaty. Sitting Bull's warriors wanted to attack the surveyors, but Sitting Bull restrained them. He hoped to work out a peaceful solution with the whites. But some of the younger, hot-headed braves, eager for a fight, ignored Sitting Bull's wishes. They slipped out in the middle of the night, stole some horses from the surveyors' camp, and triggered a battle with the soldiers. A Sioux warrior was wounded. The fighting went on for several hours. . . . Sitting Bull and Crazy Horse observed the battle from the heights. Sitting Bull saw that the fighting was evenly matched. The soldiers could not be coaxed out into the open, and the warriors could not risk charging their line.

So, Sitting Bull . . . staged a spectacle. Just as the early morning sun's rays bathed the valley in brilliant hues of gold, he gathered his pipe and tobacco pouch from his horse. He dismounted and carried his bow, arrow quiver, and rifle with him. He walked down from the bluffs to the open valley. Once out in the meadow between the two forces, he sat down and lit his pipe. He turned and called to the warriors above, inviting whomever wanted to join him to come down. Before long, four other men came forward and sat down with Sitting Bull. They puffed quietly on the pipe, passing it from one to the other. All the time, the soldiers' bullets kept whizzing by them, kicking up balls of dirt and grass. When the tobacco had all been smoked, Sitting Bull grabbed a stick, cleaned out the bowl, and put the pipe back in its pouch. He then turned and walked deliberately back to his tribesmen and told them that they had done enough fighting for one day. They all turned and left. So ended the battle of Arrow Creek. Sitting Bull's courageous act of defiance was later recounted over and over, adding to his legendary status among his people.

bluffs: high, broad-faced cliffs

Discussion Questions

1. **What effect do you think Sitting Bull's action had?**
2. **Why do you think Sitting Bull and his warriors were not hit by bullets?**
3. **Why do you think newcomers to the West killed so many buffalo? What did the buffalo mean to the Sioux?**

Encourage students to read this biography of Sitting Bull on their own.

from

Thomas Alva Edison: Bringer of Light

by Carol Greene

This excerpt from a biography of Thomas Alva Edison describes his work on the storage battery twenty years after the invention of the light bulb.

storage battery: rechargeable battery of electrochemical cells for generating electric current

economical: operating with little waste

This new idea had to do with the horseless carriage. Edison was certain that the automobile of the future would have an electric motor powered by a storage battery. He wanted to work on the storage battery.

Oddly enough, he had met a thin young man named Henry Ford a few years earlier. At that time, Ford worked in a Detroit Edison company. But he also had an idea for an automobile—one that would run on gasoline.

"Young man, that's the thing! You have it!" Edison said when Ford told him his idea.

The famous inventor's approval was great encouragement for Ford. Soon he set up his own company to make automobiles. It was just a small company then, but—

Meanwhile, though, Edison was working to perfect a storage battery for electric cars. During that period, around 1900, batteries had to be tremendously heavy to give much power. Edison's plan was to invent a lighter, more economical battery.

Once again he began thousands of experiments. By this time, of course, he had an army of scientists in his laboratory to help him. But progress was slow.

When a friend said he was sorry how badly things were going, Edison replied, "Why, man, I've got a lot of results. I know several thousand things that won't work."

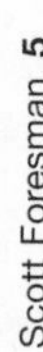

He had unusual methods of quality control, too. To test the hardness of his batteries, he had workmen throw them out of the second- and third-story windows of the laboratory!

At last, in the summer of 1904, he was ready to start manufacturing.

"It's here! The newest Edison marvel!" cried the newspapers. People gobbled up the batteries. Edison was flying high. He said: "Yes, the new battery will settle the horse—not at once but by degrees. The price of automobiles will be reduced. . . . In fact, I hope that the time has nearly arrived when every man may not only be able to light his own house, but charge his own machinery, heat his rooms, cook his food, etc., by electricity, without depending on anyone else for these services."

Then came the bad news. Many of the batteries didn't work. They leaked and they lost power. Edison didn't hesitate. He took back all the bad batteries, returned the customers' money, shut down his factory, and went back to experimenting.

It took five more years of very hard work. But in 1909, Edison could write to one of his customers, "At last the battery is finished."

Much to his disappointment, though, his battery never was used much in automobiles. That skinny young man, Henry Ford, had a better idea with his gasoline-powered cars. But people did find plenty of other uses for the Edison battery. It was used in miners' lamps, train lights, and sea machinery. It worked well for quarrying, railroad signaling, and radio telegraphy. Power stations kept Edison batteries on hand in case of emergencies and the military used them to run submarines.

Edison didn't make a lot of money from his storage battery—although he made some. But money was never important to him—at least not money for its own sake. Henry Ford once called him "the world's greatest inventor and worst businessman." Edison might have agreed.

"I always invent," he said, "to obtain money to go on inventing."

And he *did* end up a multimillionaire.

radio telegraphy: wireless system that converts a coded message into electric impulses and sends it to a receiver

Discussion Questions

1. **Why do you think Edison remained hopeful after all of his failures?**
2. **What do you think was most important to Edison in his work as an inventor? Explain your thoughts.**
3. **Have you (or someone you know) ever had an idea for an invention? Explain what it was.**

Quotes from Samuel Gompers

Samuel Gompers gave opinions on how trade unions create a better society.

arsenals: places for making or storing weapons

republican institutions: laws, customs, or practices of a government by the people

1893: We want more school houses and less jails; more books and less arsenals; more learning and less vice; more constant work and less crime; more leisure and less greed; more justice and less revenge; in fact, more of the opportunities to cultivate our better natures. . . . These in brief are the primary demands made by the Trade Unions.

1905: Any one may say that the organizations of labor invade or deny liberty to the workmen. But go to the men who worked in the bituminous coal mines twelve, fourteen, sixteen hours a day, for a dollar or a dollar and twenty five cents, and who now work eight hours a day and whose wages have increased 70 per cent in the past seven years—go tell those men that they have lost their liberty and they will laugh at you.

1891: The long hour men go home, throw themselves on a miserable apology for a bed and dream of work. They eat to work, sleep to work, and dream to work, instead of working to live. The man who goes home early has time to see his children, to eat his supper, to read the newspaper. . . . Time is the most valuable thing on earth: time to think, time to act, time to extend our fraternal relations, . . . time to become better and more independent citizens.

1900: I look to the proposition of labor to reduce the daily hours of toil of the working people of our country as the greatest proposition that has ever been offered to the Congress of the United States and to the employers of the United States; calculated to be of more benefit for the whole people of our country; calculated to be the greatest safety for the perpetuation of republican institutions, a greater safety for the progress, the success of the people of our country—all classes—of attaining a position as great and grand and successful in industry, in commerce, in intelligence, in humanity, in civilization than all the other propositions that have been submitted to this or any other previous Congress of the United States.

Discussion Questions

1. **How can trade unions help develop a civilized society?**
2. **Do you agree that improved labor conditions help maintain republican institutions? Explain.**

from

The Promised Land

by Mary Antin

In these excerpts from Mary Antin's autobiography, she describes her family's emigration from Russia, their six-week sea journey, their reunion with her father, her first impressions of home in Boston, and, finally, her wonderstruck appreciation of free school.

coveted: desired

Our turn came at last. We were conducted through the gate of departure, and after some hours of bewildering maneuvers, described in great detail in the report to my uncle, we found ourselves—we five frightened pilgrims from Polotzk—on the deck of a great big steamship afloat on the strange big waters of the ocean.

For sixteen days the ship was our world. My letter dwells solemnly on the details of the life at sea, as if afraid to cheat my uncle of the smallest circumstance. It does not shrink from describing the torments of seasickness; it notes every change in the weather. A rough night is described, when the ship pitched and rolled so that people were thrown from their berths; days and nights when we crawled through dense fogs, our foghorn drawing answering warnings from invisible ships. The perils of the sea were not minimized in the imaginations of us inexperienced voyagers. The captain and his officers ate their dinners, smoked their pipes and slept soundly in their turns, while we frightened emigrants turned our faces to the wall and awaited our watery graves. . . .

I would imagine myself all alone on the ocean, and Robinson Crusoe was very real to me. I was alone sometimes. I was aware of no human presence; I was conscious only of sea and sky and something I did not understand. And as I listened to its solemn voice, I felt as if I had found a friend, and knew that I loved the ocean. It seemed as if it were within as well as without, part of myself; and I wondered how I had lived without it, and if I could ever part with it.

And so suffering, fearing, brooding, rejoicing, we crept nearer and nearer to the coveted shore, until, on a glorious May morning, six weeks after our departure from Polotzk, our eyes beheld the Promised Land, and my father received us in his arms. . . .

ludicrous: silly

In our days of affluence in Russia we had been accustomed to upholstered parlors, embroidered linen, silver spoons and candlesticks, goblets of gold, kitchen shelves shining with copper and brass. We had featherbeds heaped halfway to the ceiling; we had clothes presses dusky with velvet and silk and fine woollen. The three small rooms into which my father now ushered us, up one flight of stairs, contained only the necessary beds, with lean mattresses; a few wooden chairs; a table or two; a mysterious iron structure, which later turned out to be a stove; a couple of unornamental kerosene lamps; and a scanty array of cooking-utensils and crockery. And yet we were all impressed with our new home and its furniture. It was not only because we had just passed through our seven lean years, cooking in earthen vessels, eating black bread on holidays and wearing cotton; it was chiefly because these wooden chairs and tin pans were American chairs and pans that they shone glorious in our eyes. And if there was anything lacking for comfort or decoration we expected it to be presently supplied—at least, we children did. Perhaps my mother alone, of us newcomers, appreciated the shabbiness of the little apartment, and realized that for her there was as yet no laying down of the burden of poverty.

Our initiation into American ways began with the first step on the new soil. My father found occasion to instruct or correct us even on the way from the pier to Wall Street, which journey we made crowded together in a rickety cab. He told us not to lean out of the windows, not to point, and explained the word "greenhorn." We did not want to be "greenhorns," and gave the strictest attention to my father's instructions. I do not know when my parents found opportunity to review together the history of Polotzk in the three years past, for we children had no patience with the subject; my mother's narrative was constantly interrupted by irrelevant questions, interjections, and explanations.

The first meal was an object lesson of much variety. My father produced several kinds of food, ready to eat, without any cooking, from little tin cans that had printing all over them. He attempted to introduce us to a queer, slippery kind of fruit, which he called "banana," but had to give it up for the time being. After the meal, he had better luck with a curious piece of furniture on runners, which he called "rocking-chair." There were five of us newcomers, and we found five different ways of getting into the American machine of perpetual motion, and many ways of getting out of it. One born and bred to the use of a rocking-chair cannot imagine how ludicrous people can make themselves when attempting to use it for the first time. We laughed immoderately over our various experiments with the novelty, which was a wholesome way of letting off steam after the unusual excitement of the day.

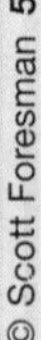

In our flat we did not think of such a thing as storing the coal in the bathtub. There was no bathtub. So in the evening of the first day my father conducted us to the public baths. As we moved along in a little procession, I was delighted with the illumination of the streets. So many lamps, and they burned until morning, my father said, and so people did not need to carry lanterns. In America, then, everything was free, as we had heard in Russia. Light was free; the streets were as bright as a synagogue on a holy day. Music was free; we had been serenaded, to our gaping delight, by a brass band of many pieces, soon after our installation on Union Place.

Education was free. That subject my father had written about repeatedly, as comprising his chief hope for us children, the essence of American opportunity, the treasure that no thief could touch, not even misfortune or poverty. It was the one thing that he was able to promise us when he sent for us; surer, safer than bread or shelter. On our second day I was thrilled with the realization of what this freedom of education meant. A little girl from across the alley came and offered to conduct us to school. My father was out, but we five between us had a few words of English by this time. We knew the word school. We understood. This child, who had never seen us till yesterday, who could not pronounce our names, who was not much better dressed than we, was able to offer us the freedom of the schools of Boston! No application made, no questions asked, no examinations, rulings, exclusions; no machinations, no fees. The doors stood open for every one of us. The smallest child could show us the way.

synagogue: building where Jews assemble for worship and study

installation: moving in

machinations: secret scheming

Discussion Questions

1. **What were some differences between the children's reactions to settling in a new country and their parents' reactions?**
2. **Why do you think Mary's father valued education above all else?**
3. **What do you think it is like to be an immigrant to the United States today? If anyone in your family was an immigrant, tell about that relative's experience.**

from

Liliuokalani: Queen of Hawaii

by Mary Malone

In this excerpt, Liliuokalani, Hawaii's last queen, gives in to the American businessmen who want her to resign.

Most of Liliuokalani's own people did support her. They were even ready to fight for her. But the queen did not want anyone to fight. She spoke to her people from the palace balcony.

"Be patient," she said. "There must be no bloodshed. For my sake, go back to your homes."

Most of them did. But some were angry about the way the queen was being treated. This gave Liliuokalani's enemies an excuse to form the Committee of Public Safety. The committee members said they feared "rioting" by the native Hawaiians. They asked the American minister in Hawaii to land troops from an American ship in Honolulu harbor. He did so.

The next day the queen looked out and saw American marines outside her palace.

"What is the meaning of this?" she asked the leader of the committee, who had come to see her.

"We are asking you to resign," he replied. "We want a businessman like Sanford Dole to head the government."

"I will not resign," Liliuokalani said. The man pointed to the guards outside. Then the queen knew that if her own people tried to help her, some might be shot. She must give in to these men. Sadly, she sat down at her desk and wrote a short note to Mr. Dole. "I am resigning," Liliuokalani said, "because I am forced to do it. To avoid the loss of life . . . I yield."

Discussion Questions

1. **What did Liliuokalani care about at this critical time?**
2. **What do you think of Liliuokalani's actions?**

from

To Build a Fire

by Jack London

In this hair-raising short story by Jack London, a gold miner hiking alone in weather 75 degrees below zero has fallen into a stream. He must light a fire to save his life.

He worked slowly and carefully, keenly aware of his danger. Gradually, as the flame grew stronger, he increased the size of the twigs with which he fed it. He squatted in the snow, pulling the twigs out from their entanglement in the brush and feeding directly to the flame. He knew there must be no failure. When it is seventy-five below zero, the man must not fail in his first attempt to build a fire—that is, if his feet are wet. If his feet are dry, and he fails, he can run along the trail for half a mile and restore his circulation. But the circulation of wet and freezing feet cannot be restored by running when it is seventy-five below. No matter how fast he runs, the wet feet will freeze the harder.

All this the man knew. The old-timer on Sulphur Creek had told him about it the previous fall, and now he was appreciating the advice. Already all sensation had gone out of his feet. To build the fire he had been forced to remove his mittens, and the fingers had quickly gone numb. His pace of four miles an hour had kept his heart pumping blood to the surface of his body and to all the extremities. But the instant he stopped, the action of the pump eased down. The cold of space smote the unprotected tip of the planet, and he, being on that unprotected tip, received the full force of the blow. The blood of his body recoiled before it. The blood was alive, like the dog, and like the dog it wanted to hide away and cover itself up from the fearful cold. So long as he walked four miles an hour, he pumped that blood, willy-nilly, to the surface, but now it ebbed away and sank down into the recesses of his body. The extremities were the first to feel its absence. His wet feet froze the faster, and his

extremities: hands and feet

smote: struck violently

recoiled: pulled back

recesses: inner places

Klondike: gold-mining region surrounding the Klondike River in northwestern Canada, near Alaska

wires were pretty well down: a metaphor comparing nerves and electric wires

exposed fingers numbed the faster, though they had not yet begun to freeze. Nose and cheeks were already freezing, while the skin of all his body chilled as it lost its blood.

But he was safe. Toes and nose and cheeks would be only touched by the frost, for the fire was beginning to burn with strength. He was feeding it with twigs the size of his finger. In another minute he would be able to feed it with branches the size of his wrist, and then he could remove his wet foot-gear, and, while it dried, he could keep his naked feet warm by the fire, rubbing them at first, of course, with snow. The fire was a success. He was safe. He remembered the advice of the old-timer on Sulphur Creek, and smiled. The old-timer had been very serious in laying down the law that no man must travel alone in the Klondike after fifty below. Well, here he was; he had had the accident; he was alone; and he had saved himself. . . . All a man had to do was to keep his head, and he was all right. Any man who was a man could travel alone. But it was surprising, the rapidity with which his checks and nose were freezing. And he had not thought his fingers could go lifeless in so short a time. Lifeless they were, for he could scarcely make them move together to grip a twig, and they seemed remote from his body and from him. When he touched a twig, he had to look and see whether or not he had hold of it. The wires were pretty well down between him and his finger-ends.

All of which counted for little. There was the fire, snapping and crackling and promising life with every dancing flame.

Discussion Questions

1. **Does the writer succeed in convincing you of how cold it is? Explain.**
2. **What do you think of the old-timer's advice?**
3. **How do you think the story will end?**

Encourage students to read the whole story, "To Build a Fire."

from

Roosevelt's Seventh Annual Address to Congress

This excerpt from Theodore Roosevelt's Seventh Annual Address to Congress expresses his deep respect for our natural resources.

earnest: promise

The conservation of our natural resources and their proper use constitute the fundamental problem which underlies almost every other problem of our National life. We must maintain for our civilization the adequate material basis without which that civilization can not exist. We must show foresight, we must look ahead. As a nation we not only enjoy a wonderful measure of present prosperity but if this prosperity is used aright it is an earnest of future success such as no other nation will have. The reward of foresight for this Nation is great and easily foretold. But there must be the look ahead, there must be a realization of the fact that to waste, to destroy, our natural resources, to skin and exhaust the land instead of using it so as to increase its usefulness, will result in undermining in the days of our children the very prosperity which we ought by right to hand down to them amplified and developed. For the last few years, through several agencies, the Government has been endeavoring to get our people to look ahead and to substitute a planned and orderly development of our resources in place of a haphazard striving for immediate profit. Our great river systems should be developed as National water highways, the Mississippi, with its tributaries, standing first in importance, and the Columbia second, although there are many others of importance on the Pacific, the Atlantic and the Gulf slopes. The National Government should undertake this work, and I hope a beginning will be made in the present Congress; and the greatest of all our rivers, the Mississippi, should receive especial attention.

Discussion Questions

1. **Did President Roosevelt want to inform or persuade his listeners? Explain.**
2. **Why do you think Teddy Roosevelt believed that conservation of natural resources was the problem at the root of all the nation's problems?**
3. **Do Roosevelt's statements remind you of present-day environmental concerns? Describe any similarities.**

from

The Panama Canal Officially Opened

This *New York Times* news article, dated August 15, 1914, celebrates the first ship's passage through the Panama Canal.

fortified islands: probably islands with military protection
discharging: offloading
manifestly: obviously

Panama, Aug 15—The Panama Canal is open to the commerce of the world. Henceforth ships may pass to and fro through that great waterway, a new ocean highway for trade thus being established.

The steamship Ancon, owned by the United States War Department and leased to the Panama Railroad for service between New York and Colon, with many notable people on board, today made the official passage which signalised the opening of the canal. She left Cristobal at 7 o'clock this morning and reached Balboa, at the Pacific end, at 4 o'clock this afternoon, having navigated the waterway in nine hours.

The Ancon did not anchor at Balboa, but proceeded into deep water in the Pacific, beyond the fortified islands, where she [will] lie in the channel of the canal until her return to Balboa to land her passengers. She will remain at the Balboa docks for some time, discharging her cargo, hers being the first commercial voyage made through the canal.

The canal having been officially opened, it will be used tomorrow for the transfer of four cargo ships, which will thus shorten their routes. The private yacht Lasata, owned in Los Angeles, also will be transferred to the Pacific, homeward bound.

The trip of the Ancon was the fastest yet made by a large ocean steamer. . . .

Col. George W. Goethals, builder of the canal and Governor of the Zone, watched the operations closely and was manifestly pleased at the improved handling of the locks. He said that even this would be made much better with time.

Discussion Questions

1. **Did this writer have firsthand knowledge of the event? What do you think this might have added to the account?**
2. **What do you think it would have been like to be a part of this historic journey?**

from

Woodrow Wilson's War Message

These excerpts from President Woodrow Wilson's War Message explain to Congress why it had become necessary for the United States to declare war on Germany.

With a profound sense of the solemn and even tragical character of the step I am taking and of the grave responsibilities which it involves, but in unhesitating obedience to what I deem my constitutional duty, I advise that the Congress declare the recent course of the Imperial German Government to be in fact nothing less than war against the Government and people of the United States; that it formally accept the status of belligerent which has thus been thrust upon it, and that it take immediate steps not only to put the country in a more thorough state of defense but also to exert all its power and employ all its resources to bring the Government of the German Empire to terms and end the war. . . .

It is a distressing and oppressive duty, gentlemen of the Congress, which I have performed in thus addressing you. There are, it may be, many months of fiery trial and sacrifice ahead of us. It is a fearful thing to lead this great peaceful people into war, into the most terrible and disastrous of all wars, civilization itself seeming to be in the balance. But the right is more precious than peace, and we shall fight for the things which we have always carried nearest our hearts—for democracy, for the right of those who submit to authority to have a voice in their own governments, for the rights and liberties of small nations, for a universal dominion of right by such a concert of free peoples as shall bring peace and safety to all nations and make the world itself at last free. To such a task we can dedicate our lives and our fortunes, everything that we are and everything that we have, with the pride of those who know that the day has come when America is privileged to spend her blood and her might for the principles that gave her birth and happiness and the peace which she has treasured. God helping her, she can do no other.

belligerent: a country recognized as being engaged in war

dominion: authority

Discussion Questions

1. **Do you think President Wilson wished to inform or persuade others? Explain.**
2. **What does President Wilson mean by "a universal dominion of right by . . . free peoples"?**

from

Crusade for Justice

by Ida B. Wells

In this excerpt from her autobiography, Ida B. Wells describes how, in 1914, she persuaded women to organize and elect local men in Illinois elections.

suffrage: the right to vote

run independent: campaigned for public office without party affiliation

alderman: member of a city council

With the assistance of one or two of my suffrage friends, I organized what afterward became known as the Alpha Suffrage Club. The women who joined were extremely interested when I showed them that we could use our vote for the advantage of ourselves and our race. We organized the block system, and once a week we met to report progress. The women at first were very much discouraged.

They said that the men jeered at them and told them they ought to be at home taking care of the babies. Others insisted that the women were trying to take the place of men and wear the trousers. I urged each one of the workers to go back and tell the women that we wanted them to register so that they could help put a colored man in the city council.

This line of argument appealed very strongly to them, since we had already taken part in several campaigns where men had run independent for alderman. The work of these women was so effective that when registration day came, the Second Ward was the sixth highest of the thirty-five wards of the city.

Our men politicians were surprised because not one of them, not even our ministers, had said one word to influence women to take advantage of the suffrage opportunity Illinois had given to her daughters.

Discussion Questions

1. **Why were the men surprised that the women worked so hard on the election campaigns?**
2. **Have you ever run for an office or helped in someone else's campaign? Tell about your experience.**

from

Lindbergh's Own Story

by Charles A. Lindbergh

In this headline story, Charles Lindbergh recounts the thoughts and emotions he had piloting solo for thrity-four hours to make the first nonstop transatlantic flight. This story appeared on the front page of the *New York Times,* May 23, 1927.

Paris, May 22—Well, here I am in the hands of American Ambassador Herrick. From what I have seen of it, I am sure I am going to like Paris.

It isn't part of my plans to fly my plane back to the United States, although that doesn't mean I have finished my flying career. If I thought that was going to be the result of my flight across the Atlantic, you may be sure I would never have undertaken it. Indeed, I hope that I will be able to do some flying over here in Europe—that is, if the souvenir hunters left enough of my plane last night.

Incidentally, that reception I got was the most dangerous part of the whole flight. If wind and storm had handled me as vigorously as that Reception Committee of Fifty Thousand I would never have reached Paris and wouldn't be eating a 3-o'clock-in-the-afternoon breakfast here in Uncle Sam's Embassy.

Uncle Sam's Embassy: the U.S. Embassy

There's one thing I wish to get straight about this flight. They call me "Lucky," but luck isn't enough. As a matter of fact, I had what I regarded and still regard as the best existing plane to make the flight from New York to Paris. I had what I regard as the best engine, and I was equipped with what were in the circumstances the best possible instruments for making such efforts. I hope I made good use of what I had.

That I landed with considerable gasoline left means that I had recalled the fact that so many flights had failed because of lack of fuel, and that was one mistake I tried to avoid.

Weather Almost Made Him Turn Back.

All in all, I couldn't complain of the weather. It wasn't what was predicted. It was worse in some places and better in others. In fact, it was so bad once that for a moment there came over me the temptation to turn back. But then I figured it was probably just as bad behind me as in front of me, so I kept on toward Paris.

throttled down: tighten a valve to reduce the flow of fuel vapor in an engine

As you know, we (that's my ship and I) took off rather suddenly. We had a report somewhere around 4 o'clock in the afternoon before that the weather would be fine, so we thought we would try it.

We had been told we might expect good weather mostly during the whole of the way. But we struck fog and rain over the coast not far from the start. Actually, it was comparatively easy to get to Newfoundland, but real bad weather began just about dark, after leaving Newfoundland, and continued until about four hours after daybreak. We hadn't expected that at all, and it sort of took us by surprise, morally and physically. That was when I began to think about turning back.

In Serious Danger From a Sleet Storm.

Then sleet began, and, as all aviators know, in a sleet storm one may be forced down in a very few minutes. It got worse and worse. There, above and below me, and on both sides, was that driving storm. I made several detours trying to get out of it, but in vain. I flew as low as ten feet above the water and then mounted up to ten thousand feet. Along toward morning the storm eased off, and I came down to a comparatively low level. . . .

I had, as I said, no trouble before I hit the storm I referred to. We had taken off at 7:55 in the morning. The field was slightly damp and soft, so the take-off was longer than it would have been otherwise. I had no trouble getting over the houses and trees. I kept out of the way of every obstacle and was careful not to take any unnecessary chances. As soon as I cleared everything, the motor was throttled down to three-fourths and kept there during the whole flight, except when I tried to climb over the storm.

Checked His Course at Newfoundland.

Soon after starting I was out of sight of land for 300 miles, from Cape Cod over the sea to Nova Scotia. The motor was acting perfectly and was carrying well the huge load of 451 gallons of gasoline and 20 gallons of oil, which gave my ship the greatest cruising radius of any plane of its type.

I passed over St. John's, N.F., purposely going out of my way a few miles to check up. I went through the narrow pass, going down so low that it could be definitely established where I was at that hour. That was the last place I saw before taking to the open sea.

I had made preparations before I started for a forced landing if it became necessary, but after I started I never thought much about the possibility of such a landing. I was ready for it, but I saw no use thinking about it, inasmuch as one place would have been about as good or as bad as another. . . .

Flew Over an Iceberg Zone.

Shortly after leaving Newfoundland I began to see icebergs. There was a low fog and even through it I could make out bergs clearly. It began to get very cold, but I was well prepared for cold. I had on ordinary flying clothing, but I was down in the cockpit, which protected me, and I never suffered from the weather.

Within an hour after the leaving the coast it became dark. Then I struck clouds and decided to try to get over them. For a while I succeeded, at a height of 10,000 feet. I flew at this height until early morning. The engine was working beautifully and I was not sleepy at all. I felt just as if I was driving a motorcar over a smooth road, only it was easier.

Then it began to get light and the clouds got higher. I went under some and over others. There was sleet in all of those clouds and the sleet began to cling to the plane. That worried me a great deal and I debated whether I should keep on or go back. I decided I must not think any more about going back. I realized that it was henceforth only a question of getting there. It was too far to turn back. . . .

The engine was working perfectly and that cheered me. I was going along a hundred miles an hour and I knew that if the motor kept on turning I would get there. After that I thought only about navigating, and then I thought that I wasn't so badly off after all. . . .

The only real danger I had was at night. In the daytime I knew where I was going, but in the evening and at night it was largely a matter of guesswork. However, my instruments were so good that I never could get more than 200 miles off my course and that was easy to correct, and I had enough extra gasoline to take care of a number of such deviations. All in all, the trip over the Atlantic, especially the latter half, was much better than I expected. . . .

"Am I on the Right Road to Ireland?"

Fairly early in the afternoon I saw a fleet of fishing boats. On some of them I could see no one, but on one of them I saw some men and flew down, almost touching the craft and yelled at them, asking if I was on the right road to Ireland.

They just stared. Maybe they didn't hear me. Maybe I didn't hear them. Or maybe they thought I was just a crazy fool.

An hour later I saw land. I have forgotten just what time it was. It must have been shortly before 4 o'clock. It was rocky land and all my study told me it was Ireland. And it was Ireland!

I slowed down and flew low enough to study the land and be sure of where I was; and believe me, it was a beautiful sight. . . .

The rest was child's play. I had my course all marked out carefully from approximately the place where I hit the coast, and you know it is quite easy to fly over strange territory if you have good maps and your course prepared.

Cherbourg: city on the west coast of France

Very lights: colored flares fired from a special pistol

Flew Low Over Ireland So He Could Be Seen.

I flew quite low enough over Ireland to be seen, but apparently no great attention was paid to me. I also flew low over England, mounted a little over the Channel and then came down close to land when I passed a little west of Cherbourg. From Cherbourg I headed for the Seine and followed it upstream.

I noticed it gets dark much later over here than in New York and I was thankful for that. What especially pleased me was the ease with which I followed my course after hitting the coast of Ireland.

When I was about half an hour away from Paris, I began to see rockets and Very lights sent up from the air field, and I knew I was all right.

Eiffel Tower Lights Come Into View.

I saw an immense vertical electric sign, which I made out to be the Eiffel Tower. I circled Paris once and immediately saw Le Bourget [the aviation field], although I didn't know at first what it was. I saw a lot of lights, but in the dark I couldn't make out any hangars. I sent Morse signals as I flew over the field, but no one appears to have seen them. The only mistake in all my calculations was that I thought Le Bourget was northeast rather than east of Paris.

Fearing for a moment that the field I had seen—remember I couldn't see the crowd—was some other airfield than Le Bourget, I flew back over Paris to the northwest, looking for Le Bourget. I was slightly confused by the fact that whereas in America when a ship is to land, beacons are put out when floodlights are turned on, at Le Bourget both beacons and floodlights were going at the same time.

I was anxious to land where I was being awaited. So when I didn't find another airfield, I flew back toward the first lights I had seen, and flying low I saw the lights of numberless automobiles. I decided that was the right place, and I landed.

Discussion Questions

1. **Why do you think Lindbergh wrote this article?**
2. **Why do you imagine Lindbergh refers to himself and his plane as "we"?**
3. **Why was the first nonstop transatlantic flight such an important event?**

Students may enjoy using online or library resources to research early airplane flight.

from

My Secret War

by Mary Pope Osborne

In these entries from a fictional diary, young Madeline Beck worries about war in the Pacific, where her father is stationed. Madeline and her mother live in a boarding house in New York, and their fellow tenants include two German Jewish refugees and a fisherman named Theo. In Madeline's class at school, a girl named Maxine leads a club of girls called the Star Points, and a boy named Johnny likes to talk with Madeline about her father and the Navy.

December 5, 1941
Dear Diary,

During social studies Mr. O'Malley quoted from a newspaper column written by Eleanor Roosevelt. Mrs. Roosevelt wants all Americans to "pledge to be a little thoughtful every day about the meaning of freedom."

Mr. O'Malley asked us each to tell the class what freedom means to us. Johnny said it meant he could read the newspaper and listen to the radio.

I said freedom meant that if I chose, I could be friends with a German Jew named Clara and no one would mind. I added that as a true friend, I would be kind and accepting and if I had a group, I would let her be part of it. I got a little carried away, I guess, trying to send a message to the Star Points.

When Maxine's turn came, she froze. She had no idea what freedom meant to her. She giggled, and like a bunch of nuts, all the Points giggled with her, changing the exercise into something silly. I thought Johnny would finally see that Maxine was an idiot. But when I looked over at him, he was laughing, too.

December 7, 1941
Dear Diary,

The Japanese have attacked us!

Theo was right—things boiled over in the Pacific!

At about 2:30 this afternoon, Mom was writing to Dad, and I was dancing to the Benny Goodman Orchestra on the radio when the announcer broke in: "Flash! The White House has reported a Japanese attack on Pearl Harbor. Japanese Imperial headquarters announces a state of war with the United States! Stay tuned for further developments!"

"Oh, my gosh!" Mom cried.

I threw open our door and shrieked to the household, "The Japanese have bombed Pearl Harbor!"

Miss Burke came out of her door, exclaiming, "What? What?" as she ran into our room, clumping in her big black shoes. "Where's Pearl Harbor?" she asked frantically.

"I don't know!" Mom said. "Maddie, find out where it is!"

I ran back into the hall and shouted over the banister, "Theo! Where's Pearl Harbor?"

Theo didn't seem to be home. As I started back to our room, I saw Clara and her mother standing in their doorway. They look[ed] scared, so I tried to speak calmly. "The Japanese have attacked a place called Pearl Harbor," I said. "We don't know where it is. But don't worry."

Mrs. Rosenthal shook her head nervously and went back into their room. Clara stayed in the hall.

I asked her if she wanted to listen to our radio. She said she'd better not leave her mother. I told her I'd come give her reports.

At that moment, Theo came through the front door, and I hollered the news to him.

When Theo joined Mom, Miss Burke, and me, he told us that Pearl Harbor was in Hawaii. Miss Burke didn't believe him until the radio confirmed that Pearl Harbor was on the Hawaiian island of Oahu.

Mom and I were nearly hysterical, worrying that Dad's ship might have been at Pearl Harbor. It was a relief when the announcer finally said that hundreds of ships were destroyed or damaged, but none of them were aircraft carriers. Mom grabbed me and hugged me, and we both laughed. It was terrible of us, but we were momentarily so happy—one thing we know for sure is that Dad is on an aircraft carrier.

Discussion Questions

1. **Why does Madeline believe that choosing friends is part of freedom?**
2. **If someone asked you what freedom meant to you, what would you say?**

from

Eisenhower's First Inaugural Address

In this inaugural speech, given January 20, 1953, President Dwight David Eisenhower tells our nation's citizenry that we are at a turning point in history.

My fellow citizens:

The world and we have passed the midway point of a century of continuing challenge. We sense with all our faculties that forces of good and evil are massed and armed and opposed as rarely before in history.

This fact defines the meaning of this day. We are summoned by this honored and historic ceremony to witness more than the act of one citizen swearing his oath of service, in the presence of God. We are called as a people to give testimony in the sight of the world to our faith that the future shall belong to the free.

Since this century's beginning, a time of tempest has seemed to come upon the continents of the earth. Masses of Asia have awakened to strike off shackles of the past. Great nations of Europe have fought their bloodiest wars. Thrones have toppled and their vast empires have disappeared. New nations have been born.

For our own country, it has been a time of recurring trial. We have grown in power and in responsibility. We have passed through the anxieties of depression and of war to a summit unmatched in man's history. Seeking to secure peace in the world we have had to fight through the forests of the Argonne, to the shores of Iwo Jima, and to the cold mountains of Korea. . . .

How far have we come in man's long pilgrimage from darkness toward light? Are we nearing the light—a day of freedom and of peace for all mankind? Or are the shadows of another night closing in upon us? . . .

At such a time in history, we who are free must proclaim anew our faith. This faith is the abiding creed of our fathers. It is our faith in the deathless dignity of man, governed by eternal moral and natural laws.

This faith defines our full view of life. It establishes, beyond debate, those gifts of the Creator that are man's inalienable rights, and that make all men equal in His sight.

In the light of this equality, we know that the virtues most cherished by free people—love of truth, pride of work, devotion to country—all are treasures equally precious in the lives of the most humble and of the most exalted. The men who mine coal and fire

time of tempest: violent period

Argonne: wooded region in northeast France, where Americans fought Germans in World War I

Iwo Jima: Pacific island where Americans fought Japanese in World War II

abiding: lasting

inalienable: incapable of being taken away or transferred

ledger: book of accounts
bar: any place of judgment
precepts: rules of conduct

furnaces and balance ledgers and turn lathes and pick cotton and heal the sick and plant corn—all serve as proudly, and as profitably, for America as the statesmen who draft treaties and the legislators who enact laws.

This faith rules our whole way of life. It decrees that we, the people, elect leaders not to rule but to serve. It asserts that we have the right to choice of our own work and to the reward of our own toil. It inspires the initiative that makes our productivity the wonder of the world. And it warns that any man who seeks to deny equality among all his brothers betrays the spirit of the free and invites the mockery of the tyrant. . . .

We feel this moral strength because we know that we are not helpless prisoners of history. We are free men. We shall remain free, never to be proven guilty of the one capital offense against freedom, a lack of stanch faith.

In pleading our just cause before the bar of history and in pressing our labor for world peace, we shall be guided by certain fixed principles. . . .

We must be ready to dare all for our country. For history does not long entrust the care of freedom to the weak or the timid. We must acquire proficiency in defense and display stamina in purpose.

We must be willing, individually and as a Nation, to accept whatever sacrifices may be required of us. A people that values its privileges above its principles soon loses both.

These basic precepts are not lofty abstractions, far removed from matters of daily living. . . . Patriotism means equipped forces and a prepared citizenry. Moral stamina means more energy and more productivity. . . . Love of liberty means the guarding of every resource that makes freedom possible. . . .

And so each citizen plays an indispensable role. The productivity of our heads, our hands, and our hearts is the source of all the strength we can command, for both the enrichment of our lives and winning of the peace.

No person, no home, no community can be beyond the reach of this call. We are summoned to act in wisdom and in conscience, to work with industry, to teach with persuasion, to preach with conviction, to weigh our every deed with care and with compassion. For this truth must be clear before us: whatever America hopes to bring to pass in the world must first come to pass in the heart of America.

Discussion Questions

1. **What does President Eisenhower mean by "faith" in this speech?**
2. **Do you agree that faith supports freedom? Explain.**

from

The Autobiography of Malcolm X

These two excerpts show that Malcolm X thought of racism as a black problem before his pilgrimage to Mecca and as a human problem when he came back home.

The American black man should be focusing his every effort toward building his *own* businesses, and decent homes for himself. As other ethnic groups have done, let the black people, wherever possible, however possible, patronize their own kind, hire their own kind, and start in those ways to build up the black race's ability to do for itself. That's the only way the American black man is ever going to get respect. One thing the white man never can give the black man is self-respect! The black man never can become independent and recognized as a human being who is truly equal with other human beings until he has what they have, and until he is doing for himself what others are doing for themselves. . . .

I said that on the American racial level, we had to approach the black man's struggle against the white man's racism as a human problem, that we had to forget hypocritical politics and propaganda. I said that both races, as human beings, had the obligation, the responsibility, of helping to correct America's human problem. The well-meaning white people, I said, had to combat, actively and directly, the racism in other white people. And the black people had to build within themselves much greater awareness that along with equal rights there had to be the bearing of equal responsibilities.

patronize: to support or sponsor

hypocritical: insincere

propaganda: widespread promotion of ideas to further one's own cause or damage another's

Discussion Questions

1. **How would you describe the differences between Malcolm X's thinking in the two excerpts?**
2. **Why do you think Malcolm X might have changed his approach?**

from

Cesar Chavez: Man of Courage

by Florence M. White

In this excerpt from her biography of Cesar Chavez, Florence White describes how consumers and truckers from California to Sweden began to support Chavez's union through a boycott.

Delano: farming town in California's San Joaquin Valley
huelga: strike (Spanish)

In the spring of 1968 most grape growers still had refused to meet with Cesar. They brought in workers from other countries to break the strike.

"Then we will take our strike to other countries," Cesar told the strikers. "We will ask people everywhere not to buy grapes—to boycott them until the strike is settled and every box of grapes carries a union label."

Soon strikers and volunteers who had picketed the vineyards of Delano rode across the country in old cars or on freight trains. They planned to picket the supermarkets all over the United States and across the border in Canada.

With signs reading, "Don't buy grapes," "Huelga, Yes! Grapes, No!" "Help the Grape Strikers," they picketed stores in Washington, New York, and other large cities. Thousands of Americans joined them on the picket lines.

Cesar traveled across the country. He spoke to large meetings at churches, colleges, union halls. He appeared on television. "Don't buy grapes," he pleaded.

Many truck drivers refused to deliver grapes. Mayors of some large cities ordered their city cafeterias to stop buying grapes. Unions in England and Sweden urged their members not to unload shipments of grapes.

The growers became worried. Several signed contracts, but many still refused. . . .

During the five years of the strike, many Americans, troubled by the suffering of farm workers, had tried to help the owners and the strikers come to an agreement. But most of the owners would not take their advice.

Finally a committee of the National Conference of Catholic Bishops came. They spoke with many vineyard owners. At last the owners agreed to meet with Cesar.

On July 29, 1970, before 400 cheering farm workers, Cesar signed contracts with most of the vineyards of California. It was the biggest victory for farm workers in the history of America.

Cesar Chavez' brave struggle had given hope to over three million farm workers in the United States. . . .

Cesar's first promise to his people came true. The farm workers had a union, the first successful farm workers' union in America. Grape workers earned two dollars an hour. They got work through the union hiring hall instead of through labor contractors. The most dangerous insect poisons were no longer used. A health plan was set up and named after Senator Robert F. Kennedy. Every box of grapes was stamped with the union label, the black Aztec eagle. Most important of all, the United Farm Workers Organizing Committee acted for the farm workers in all their dealings with the growers.

Discussion Questions

1. **How would you describe the writer's attitude towards Cesar Chavez?**
2. **In what ways do you think the farm workers were treated poorly by the growers before there was a union?**
3. **Why was Chavez able to overcome the growers through peaceful demonstrations?**

from

The End of the War to End Wars

In an editorial printed November 11, 1989, the *New York Times* defines this moment as the end of a 75-year struggle that started before World War I.

convulsed: shook
Continent's: belonging to Europe
stasis: stoppage of flow
dissolution: breaking apart
polarized: separated into opposed groups
Mikhail Gorbachev: Soviet premier from 1985 to 1991

Crowds of young Germans danced on top of the hated Berlin wall Thursday night. They danced for joy, they danced for history. They danced because the tragic cycle of catastrophes that first convulsed Europe 75 years ago, embracing two world wars, a Holocaust and a cold war, seems at long last to be nearing an end. . . .

Some 20 million people died in World War I, perhaps 50 million in World War II, but even these two appalling acts of miscalculation and bloodletting did not bring Europe's torments to an end. The tragedy had a third act: the cold war divided a Europe freed from Hitler's tyranny from a Europe bowed under Stalin's. The Berlin wall, erected by Erich Honecker in 1961, stood as the foremost symbol of that division and the Continent's continuing stasis.

The reveling crowds of Berliners mingling from East and West could scarcely believe that the hated wall had at last been breached. Those watching them around the world could only share their delight—and their wonder at the meaning of it all.

If the horrifying cycle that began in 1914 is at last completed, what new wheels have begun to turn? Instability in Eastern Europe has seldom brought good news. But this dissolution may lead to settlement, even if the settlement's shape remains unclear.

Armistice is only the laying down of arms, not peace. And for as long as it has stood, the Berlin wall has symbolized a Europe not at peace, and a world polarized by Soviet-American rivalry.

Mikhail Gorbachev has spoken of a European house. No one, not even he, can yet be sure how the rooms might fit together. Still, no house has a wall through the middle, and for the first time in a generation, neither does Europe.

Discussion Questions

1. **How does this piece differ from a news article?**
2. **Why does the editorial writer think the fall of the Berlin Wall is so important?**

from

One Day in Math Class

by Taylor Sweeny Barash

Taylor Sweeny Barash was eleven years old and had just started sixth grade in a school in lower Manhattan when the World Trade Center was attacked on September 11, 2001. This is part of her account of that day.

We were in math class and it was very boring and then we heard a huge boom. Apparently, it was the second plane that hit the towers. I thought it was some construction going on and they were breaking down a building to rebuild a new one. My classmates had seen people running and screaming on the street. When I looked, I saw a flood of police cars, fire trucks and ambulances. . . . We couldn't concentrate on our assignment, so Chiman our Math teacher brought us to the rug to discuss our feelings. . . .

Then we heard over the PA system our gym teacher saying, "Be calm, don't panic, just don't panic, we really need you to stay calm, everyone stay away from the south end of the building." I didn't know which end of the building was the south end. That made it even scarier for me. A lady came in to our class and announced that a plane had flown into the World Trade Center. . . . On our way down to the cafeteria, Jade told me he saw the plane crash into the WTC from science class. At first I didn't believe him, but Dyl (a friend of mine and a classmate of Jade's) told me and I believed her.

In the cafeteria, kids were being picked up by the minute. At one point Ann was sobbing. Audra, our literacy teacher, asked Hannah and me if we needed a hug and we both accepted. And everyone kept trying to convince us that everything was OK.

Discussion Questions

1. **What do you think of this first-person account? How do you think Taylor felt?**
2. **What are some reasons why someone would want to record their experience of this event?**
3. **How do you think Taylor reacted to people "trying to convince us that everything was OK"?**

Students may want to discuss their own reactions to the September 11 attacks.

from

George W. Bush's Address to Congress

President George W. Bush gave this speech to Congress and the American people on September 20, 2001.

mission: special task or purpose
rally: gather
falter: stumble
course: onward movement from one to the next

After all that has just passed—all the lives taken, and all the possibilities and hopes that died with them—it is natural to wonder if America's future is one of fear. Some speak of an age of terror. I know there are struggles ahead, and dangers to face. But this country will define our times, not be defined by them. As long as the United States of America is determined and strong, this will not be an age of terror; this will be an age of liberty, here and across the world.

Great harm has been done to us. We have suffered great loss. And in our grief and anger we have found our mission and our moment. Freedom and fear are at war. The advance of human freedom—the great achievement of our time, and the great hope of every time—now depends on us. Our nation—this generation—will lift a dark threat of violence from our people and our future. We will rally the world to this cause by our efforts, by our courage. We will not tire, we will not falter, and we will not fail.

It is my hope that in the months and years ahead, life will return almost to normal. We'll go back to our lives and routines, and that is good. Even grief recedes with time and grace. But our resolve must not pass. Each of us will remember what happened that day, and to whom it happened. We'll remember the moment the news came—where we were and what we were doing. . . .

The course of this conflict is not known, yet its outcome is certain. Freedom and fear, justice and cruelty, have always been at war, and we know that God is not neutral between them.

Fellow citizens, we'll meet violence with patient justice—assured of the rightness of our cause, and confident of the victories to come. In all that lies before us, may God grant us wisdom, and may He watch over the United States of America.

Discussion Questions

1. **What do you think President Bush wanted to accomplish with this speech?**
2. **What do you think President Bush means by "meet violence with patient justice"?**